Chris
you probab
ly have visited ...
Love
Rud

Waterfalls
of
Massachusetts

An Explorer's Guide to
55 Natural Scenic Wonders

Trail directions, notes and photographs by
Joseph Bushee Jr.

with
supplementary text by
Valerie Vaughan

2004
New England Cartographics
North Amherst, Massachusetts
www.necartographics.com

Cover design by Valerie Vaughan
Cover photo of Royalston Falls by Joseph Bushee Jr.

New England Cartographics   OR   Joseph Bushee Jr.
PO Box 9369   2 Gunn St.
North Amherst MA 01059   Erving MA 01344
email: geolopes@crocker.com   joe@massfalls.com

Library of Congress Control # 2004101147
Manufactured in the United States of America
ISBN 1-889787-12-4

Trail guide text and photographs by Joseph Bushee Jr.
Additional text, editing, typesetting and layout by Valerie Vaughan

Trail Maps courtesy of the USGS, *www.usgs.gov*

10 9 8 7 6 5 4 3 2 1   10 09 08 07 06 05 04

Attention Readers!
*** Due to potential changes in trail conditions,
the use of information in this book is at the sole risk of the user.
* Some trails may cross through portions of private land
and may not always be open to the public.
Please respect the rights of owners.**

---

*We welcome reader feedback concerning the walks in this book.
Please send corrections, comments and suggestions to*
New England Cartographics, PO Box 9369, North Amherst MA 01059

Acknowledgments

I would like to thank my family and friends who gave me support and encouragement throughout this project. Who listened to my ramblings about walking and waterfalls and exposures with apparent interest, and never a yawn.

I'd especially like to thank my wife Ann, and my son Jake, who accompanied me on the many miles of trail, looking for falls to add to this guide, without complaint for the duds and wrong turns along the way... Well, almost.

Foreword

Thank you for your interest in *Waterfalls of Massachusetts,* my little collection of short trips to some pretty cool places here in Massachusetts. Look around. Try out some of the guided walks. Let me know what you think. I hope you'll enjoy them as much as I did. After wading in the bit-stream all week long, it's nice to get out and enjoy a real one on the weekends.

I wrote this book primarily to share my love of the outdoors, and also to provide a destination. What better destination than a scenic waterfall? Hopefully, these cool destinations will draw readers in, and encourage them to get out of the house and enjoy these natural scenic wonders of Massachusetts.

If you have questions or comments, or if you find errors, or know of other suitable waterfalls to add to my collection, don't hesitate to email me at : joe @ massfalls.com -- or visit my web site *www.massfalls.com*

Joseph Bushee Jr

Contents

The Geology and History of Waterfalls   6
Equipment and Safety   15
How to Use This Guide   18

The Geology and History of Waterfalls

Great Accidents of Erosion

However it may be formed, a waterfall is an aberration. Ordinarily, a river expends its energy more or less steadily, and not too much in any one place along its route. But at a waterfall, great quantities of energy are dissipated at an extravagant rate. However, as soon as a waterfall is formed, water power goes to work to erode the falls and restore the river's original (less steep) bed.

Waterfalls are temporary features of streams because these are locations where stream erosion is greatest. One way in which streams erode at waterfalls is by undermining. The water falling into the plunge pool at the base of the waterfall erodes the rock there, leaving rocks at the top of the falls to overhang. From time to time, pieces break off the top. Each time this occurs, the waterfall recedes farther upstream. The rate of undermining and recession is fastest when the rocks contain fractures or are poorly cemented.

Erosion in the plunge pool of a waterfall.

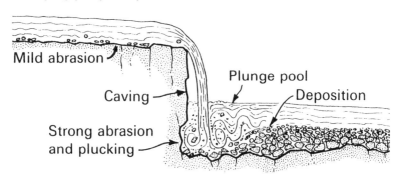

Mild abrasion

Caving

Plunge pool

Deposition

Strong abrasion
and plucking

The mechanics of erosion

The extreme turbulence along steep cascades and at waterfalls gives the water tremendous erosive power. The swirling currents may pluck and carry away large blocks of bedrock from the brink of the waterfall. Water falling freely is accelerated by gravity at a rate of about 9.8 meters per second. At Niagara Falls, the water carrying rock debris strikes the base of the 50-meter-high fall at about 80 kilometers per hour. It scours deep plunge pools that undermine the rock beneath the lip of the fall, making it susceptible to caving. Thus, undercutting at the plunge pool, along with caving of the walls, contribute greatly to the erosion of some stream valleys.

6

Section across a waterfall, showing the sequence of hard and soft formations and illustrating the mechanism of recession.

The Geology of Waterfalls

As a stream cuts its channel deeper, it is likely to encounter rocks with differing degrees of resistance to erosion. The softer rock layers erode more easily but harder layers tend to remain, impeding the stream and creating waterfalls. In many places, a flowing stream finds a softer portion of rock or sometimes a crack or other area of weakness, and it carves for itself a narrow channel known as a gorge. Gorges contain cascades of tumbling water, but they differ from waterfalls in being essentially linear with steep walls. In contrast, waterfalls are short, with a vertical or near-vertical drop of water.

What distinguishes a waterfall is its verticality. A waterfall is a vertical or nearly vertical section in the longitudinal profile of a river or stream. The erosional activity undercuts the falls and causes them to migrate upstream.

Where resistant rock is followed downstream by a weaker formation, the latter is worn down. Where a bed of strong rock (horizontal or gently inclined) overlies weaker beds, the former is the "fall-maker," and the scouring of the softer beds underneath leads to undermining and recession. The Niagara Falls are a classic example of this.

7

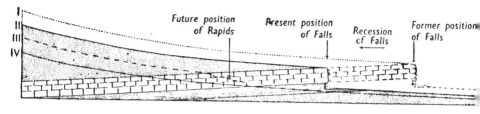

Successive stages in the recession and elimination of a waterfall

I   Profile of stream (drawn as graded) above an early position of the falls
II Present profile above falls
III Future profile after degeneration of the falls into rapids
IV Future profile (graded throughout) after elimination of falls and rapids

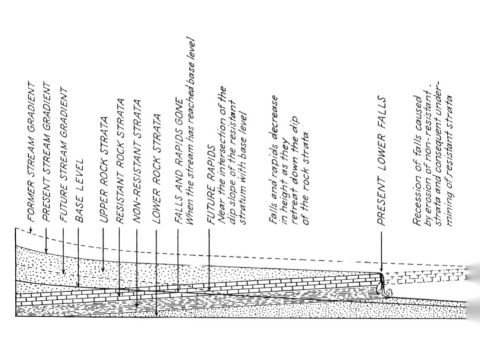

A diagram to illustrate the cause of waterfalls in gently inclined sedimentary rocks and the reason why such falls retreat upstream, leaving a gorge, and eventually disappear.

The History Surrounding
the Waterfalls of Massachusetts

As you follow the guided walks in this book, you will come across two common features of the Massachusetts countryside: stone walls and old mill foundations. The following section offers some historical background so that you might better appreciate what you encounter on your visits to the waterfalls.

Written in Stone

Anyone who ventures out into the woods of Massachusetts won't travel far before encountering a stone wall. And it nearly always comes as a surprise. Just when you are deep in the forest, surrounded by that wild peacefulness, and you begin to imagine that you are treading ground where no human has walked before -- you suddenly come upon a carefully built stone wall. Thinking to yourself that this must be an anomaly, or some kind of unusual occurrence, you move on, only to encounter another stone wall, and then another ...

It's hard to believe, but these seemingly out-of-place stone walls run nearly everywhere in Massachusetts (as well as throughout all of New England). They are the solid evidence of how extensively the land was once cultivated. Only 150 years ago, more than 75% of the land was cleared and farmed. How many miles of stone walls are there? In 1871, the U.S. Department of Agriculture conducted a survey and issued a report entitled *Statistics of Fences in the United States*. The results were -- and still *are* -- astounding. In Massachusetts, there were 33,000 miles of fencing, and nearly half were stone walls.

That's over 15,000 miles of stone walls! And most are still standing. Let's put this figure in perspective. Massachusetts is a small state; it measures only about 150 miles from east to west and only 50 miles north to south -- a total of 7,838 square miles. Thus, on average, every square mile of Massachusetts land contains about two miles of stone walls.

Another way to look at this is from the labor perspective. An average-sized 19th century farm of 130 acres was subdivided by an average of five miles of stone walls. One commonly used estimate is that two men could build ten feet of stone wall per day (that includes the time required to gather stones, move them, and lay the foundation). At that rate, it would have taken two men working every day for seven years to lay the walls on this average farm. Of course, the weather, the seasons, and the necessary operations of running a farm would not allow such continuous wall-building, so it must have taken decades to complete the job. What a monument to Yankee determination and dedication to work!

Water-Powered Mills of Old New England

Waterfalls are generally considered to be scenic natural wonders, but the fact is that in Massachusetts, they have historical significance as well, due to their role in the Industrial Revolution as the common site for mills. The widespread nature of mills is evident in the names of streets, rivers, ponds, and even the waterfalls themselves. Numerous towns in Massachusetts have a "Mill River," many have a "Mill Street," and there is even a town named after its waterfall, "Miller's Falls." Many of the waterfalls listed in this guide are located at the site of an old mill (See page 12).

There are about 4,000 mill dams still standing in Massachusetts, a sign of how important mills were in the development and early settlement of New England. Gristmills and sawmills were always built beside reliable rivers and streams, usually near waterfalls. Many rivers had to be dammed so that millponds could be created to act as reservoirs, enabling the mills to continue operating even when the river levels were down. The construction of these mills was often considered to be the first sign of civilization, and their existence led to community development, attracting more settlers and merchants.

Water-powered mills were once the nucleus of most New England industrial communities. Throughout the 19th century, they were ubiquitous on the Massachusetts landscape, but today it is unusual to find mill buildings with their large waterwheels intact. In the early 20th century, the widespread development of electric power made the mills obsolete. The nostalgia evoked by this transition is recorded in the song "Down by the Old Mill Stream" (see page 12). If there were any buildings left standing at these abandoned mills, most were knocked down by the destructive Hurricane of 1938. Finally, any mills that survived into the second half of the 20th century fell victim to new building reconstruction, or have been converted into homes, shops, or restaurants.

The water-powered gristmills and sawmills that dotted local rivers and streams during colonial times were usually owned by partnerships. Many had been granted water privileges on the condition that they would provide custom services to the local residents. Although some of these operations bought grain or wool for processing and sale, they often worked as a custom mill, charging a toll for processing materials brought to them by local households. From the 1790s onward, carding and fulling machines were installed at many sites to process wool and cloth for local spinners and weavers.

Virtually all mills advertised their services in exchange for farm produce as well as cash payment. Much of the work of constructing and equipping the mills, including simple workshops and tools, was carried out by local residents.

At the time of the 1810 census, there were 57 carding machines and 67 fulling mills scattered throughout Hampshire County, almost one-third of the total number in Massachusetts. Several of the mill sites served different functions in different seasons. Carding mills ran in the summer after sheep shearing. The gristmill season peaked in the autumn and early winter, following the harvest. Sawmills worked from early spring onward, after farmers had cleared land and brought lumber in for cutting while snow was on the ground. Fulling took place in the spring and early summer, when households sent in cloth for dressing which they had made during the winter.

Curiously, it was not access to navigable rivers nor good roads that played the major role in where these mill sites were located. What was important was access to local raw materials, local credit within a reciprocal exchange network, and most of all, the availability of labor. Thus, the sights and sounds of the mills could be found throughout the entire countryside of Massachusetts.

The Preservation of Old Mills

For those interested in the history and preservation of mills, there is the Northeast Chapter of the Society for the Preservation of Old Mills (SPOOM), which puts out a newsletter concerning tours and restoration efforts of buildings that were once an important part of the country's economy. One of the challenges of preserving mills in the United States is finding someone who knows how to restore them to working operation. The *SPOOM Northeaster*, includes a column that answers technical questions from millwrights -- people who maintain the buildings' mechanical equipment.

One reason to preserve old mills is that milled flour tastes better than its commercial counterpart. When grain is milled slowly (as it is in old mills), at about 80 r.p.m., the fiber content isn't broken down as much as when it is milled industrially. Also, when the grain is ground more quickly (as it is in modern mills), it is heated to a higher temperature. When it is heated to more than 120 degrees, the enzymes and vitamins are destroyed. This is one reason why commercial flour has to be "enriched" with artificially added nutrients.

Interested readers can visit the historic Wayside Inn gristmill in Sudbury, Massachusetts, which was originally built in 1740 and then rebuilt in 1929. The inn's bakery features products made with the mill's stone-ground wheat and corn. There are other working wheel-powered mills located on Cape Cod – the Dexter Mill in Sandwich and the Stoney Brook Grist Mill in Brewster.

Down by the Old Mill Stream

Words and Music by Tell Taylor, 1910

My darling I am dreaming of the days gone by,
When you and I were sweethearts beneath the summer sky;
Your hair has turned to silver the gold has faded too;
But still I will remember, where I first met you.

The old mill wheel is silent and has fallen down,
The old oak tree has withered and lies there on the ground;
While you and I are sweethearts the same as days of yore;
Although we've been together, forty years and more.

Chorus:

> Down by the old mill stream
>   where I first met you,
> With your eyes of blue,
>   dressed in gingham too,
> It was there I knew
>   that you loved me true,
> You were sixteen,
>   my village queen,
> Down by the old mill stream.

Waterfalls in this guidebook
that are located near old mill sites:

Sage's Ravine Brook	(# 2)	Hudson Brook Chasm	(# 21)
Glendale Falls	(# 25)	Slatestone Brook	(# 29)
Chapel Falls	(# 33)	Turkey Hill Brook	(# 41)
Lovellville Falls	(# 42)	Doane Falls	(# 45)
Noanet Brook	(# 50)	Danforth Falls	(# 51)
Beaver Brook	(# 52)	Powwow River	(# 55)

Waterfall Worship and Mythology

To many people and cultures of the world (past and present), the waters of the earth are sacred. Waterfalls, like springs or lakes or wells, are considered the home of nature deities. Some water worshippers have believed that spirit makes the thundering noise of the falling water, or that the waters themselves have healing power.

In Celtic myths, spirits cured with the power of water from waterfalls; in African myths, spirits in waterfalls can make sick children healthy. In Japan, there is a waterfall god Fudo who had a shrine on the slope of Mount Shiratake and had the ability to cure blindness.

To the North American Iroquois, Niagara Falls represented an extraordinary manifestation of spirit in nature. The name Niagara meant "thundering water," and the Iroquois explained the rushing noise as the voice of the water spirit.

Perhaps the best known waterfall legend in Massachusetts is the story of Bash Bish Falls (# 1).

The Legend of Bash Bish Falls

Before the white man came to North America, many Algonquin tribes populated the northeast, among them the Mohicans of western Massachusetts. Within their society, polygamy was not uncommon and divorce was frequently allowed. Adultery, however, was an intolerable offense and was punishable by death.

This legend revolves around a beautiful Mohican woman named Bash-Bish who was accused of adultery, the gravest of crimes, was found guilty and condemned to death as prescribed by tribal law -- despite her persistent protestations of innocence. For the execution of her sentence, a canoe equipped with leather thongs was secured in the swift water upstream from a waterfall. Bash-Bish was to be bound to the vessel, which was then to be released and drawn by the current over the fateful cataract.

At the appointed hour, the members of the tribe solemnly gathered for the ceremony. Among them was White Swan, the infant daughter of Bash Bish.

13

Suddenly, a curious thing happened. A fine mist began to surround the area, and a ring of bright butterflies circled Bash-Bish's head. As the Mohicans fell back in awe of the unexplained phenomenon, the condemned woman broke free, dashed to the edge of the waterfalls and flung herself over the waterfall, the butterflies spiralling downward behind her. Her body disappeared and was never found in the pool below.

To the Indians, this mysterious avoidance of their official punishment was a negative sign. It meant that Bash Bish was in league with evil spirits, and she was posthumously pronounced a witch. Her daughter, however, was not likewise condemned, but rather was adopted by the tribe.

White Swan grew to be as lovely as her mother and in time married a handsome clansman, son of the ruling chief. They were a devoted couple, but White Swan found she was unable to bear children. The husband, in keeping with tradition, took a second wife to give him an heir. Immediately, sorrow overwhelmed White Swan, and she began to languish. She took to brooding on a crag above the falls, and even though her husband would bring her gifts and adornments of nuts and shells from the far-away sea, her dark melancholy increased.

One night, White Swan dreamed that Bash-Bish was beckoning to her from beyond the waterfall, pleading with her to leave earthly woes behind and join her. To Mohicans, dreams proclaimed prophetic truth, and for the next few days White Swan never left the crag. Gazing down the long watery precipice to the blue-green depths below, she awaited her mother's next call.

The awaited message came one evening just as White Swan's husband emerged from the forest bearing the most beautiful gift he could find, a pure white butterfly. Gently he spoke her name, but the enraptured girl did not hear. As he watched in horror, she suddenly plunged toward the falls, and as his hands flew open in shock, the released butterfly followed White Swan's falling figure. In a vain attempt to save her, he too leaped into the water. The following day his broken body was found, but there was not a trace of White Swan, now reunited forever with her mother behind the glittering waterfall.

The site is now set aside as Bash-Bish State Forest where to this day the cascading water sometimes assumes the unmistakable shape of a woman, and on moonlit nights, a smiling female face may be seen beneath the surface of the pool below.

Equipment and Safety

To make your waterfall trip more enjoyable, safe and productive, here are some important factors to keep in mind.

Clothing and Footwear

Wear clothes you don't mind getting dirty since they are bound to get dirty. Wear sturdy boots since many waterfall trails are muddy, and some require crossing a stream. It is quite easy to get wet while visiting a waterfall, so it's a good idea to bring along a spare pair of socks and shoes. You might also consider bringing a change of clothes. And speaking of getting wet from waterfall spray, some good protection is afforded by a lightweight rain poncho. Remember, the weather in Massachusetts can change quickly. Be prepared with gloves, hat, an extra layer, or rain gear.

What Else to Bring

Water - *Always* bring water, and *never* drink untreated water from streams.

Food - Waterfalls are great spots for picnics. Enjoy your meal, but please, do not leave leftover food, assuming that wild animals will "take care of it." All garbage and trash, including food and packaging, should be removed when you leave and be disposed of properly. Scenic wonders such as waterfalls do not necessarily provide garbage cans for your personal convenience, so it's a good idea to bring along a plastic bag to use for carrying out trash. And if you'd like to do a good deed, you can also use the bag for picking up the litter that less considerate people have left along trails.

Camera - With the changing nature of waterfalls, there's great possibilities for a variety of pictures. See page 17 for photography suggestions.

Notepad and pen - Poets have been inspired by waterfalls, but so have artists; so you might consider bringing a sketch pad and portable watercolor paints.

Insect repellent - You may not always need it, but when you do, you'll be so glad you brought it. Streamside environments can be buggy.

Day-pack - Your trips will be greatly enhanced by carrying a small day-pack or fanny-pack containing a few essentials. The most common items will include a water bottle, some food, pocket knife, map and compass, small flashlight, first aid kit, length of cord, rain gear, tissues or toilet paper, and extra clothing. You might also opt to bring sunscreen, glasses or personal needs such as medication.

Miscellaneous Suggestions

Allow extra time. You never know whether the lighting might be perfect for extra camera shots, or if the good weather will inspire you to explore nearby trails. If you have limited time to visit waterfalls, don't rush around trying to get in as many waterfalls as possible. Plan carefully, pick a few, and spend your time appreciating the falls instead of driving in the car.

Be courteous to other waterfall visitors. Most people visit waterfalls for peace, quiet and natural beauty. Noisy groups, wailing babies, splashing swimmers, or pushy photographers can disrupt that peace and can ruin someone else's visit. In this age of "multiple use," there are bound to be "user conflicts," so everyone has to allow others to have their turn. Please be reasonable and aware of others. That goes for smoking, too, which can ruin the atmosphere of fresh air. Portable radios, CD players or similar noise makers are completely inappropriate in natural surroundings. Cell phones may be useful for emergencies, but they are disruptive and should be turned off or left in your vehicle.

An important point to remember: Trails should never be taken for granted as just somehow *being* there. Somebody, or some group, is responsible for trail making and maintenance. Please support the organizations that help keep the paths open to waterfalls. They are listed at the end of this guide in "Resources."

Safety Tips

Bring this guidebook as well as any supplementary maps or directions. A compass is also useful. It is highly advisable to read through the directions and trail notes prior to embarking on your waterfall trip. This will give you clues as to what kind of terrain to expect (and thus, appropriate shoes or clothing), how long it will take (and thus, how much water or food to bring), etc.

From a safety standpoint, it is best not to hike alone. However, whether you venture out alone or in company, it is advisable to inform someone back at home of exactly where you are going, and when you can be expected to return.

No matter how clean, clear, and inviting that stream water looks, *don't drink it!*

Be cautious near waterfalls. Wet rocks are slippery. Currents in streams can be deceptively fast. Swimming, diving or wading spots can appear deceptively deep (or shallow). Be careful when rockhopping. Don't climb on cliffs unless you are an experienced rock climber and have landowner permission.

Swimming (where allowed) should only be done in calm pools *below* waterfalls and never *above* a waterfall. Remember also that all stream water is much colder than you think. In the winter, avoid walking on ice-covered streams and ponds.

Advice for Photographers

Use a single-lens-reflex camera; its most important advantage is the ability to use a slow shutter speed. A shutter speed of 1/8 second or slower will blur the falling water, creating the soft streaming effect of professional waterfall photography. This effect is more pronounced with lower water volumes. Sometimes, a very high shutter speed to stop the motion creates an interesting effect as well.

Use a tripod. Handholding a shot with a slow shutter speed often blurs the picture. A tripod will keep the picture sharp. A cable release for the shutter will also prevent any unnecessary shaking of the camera as it takes the photograph.

Use good film with a low ISO (speed of the film). ISO of 100 or lower allows you to take photographs with a shutter speed of 1/8 second or slower in many light conditions. It also gives you a fine grain in your pictures which allows for higher quality enlargements. The speed of negative film only goes down to 100 ISO, so if you wish to use a slower speed film, you will have to use slide film.

Overcast skies are desirable. The sun gives photos a spark but will also make it harder to get a slow shutter speed because of the extra light. Sometimes in the forest, the sun will throw shadows on the waterfall, making it look odd.

Overexpose one or two stops. The white water in a waterfall can cause the camera's light meter to register a value which will make the water look gray rather than white. To solve this, open up a stop or two, or take pictures at several different exposure settings. This also helps when you are including people in the photograph.

Use a polarizing and/or warming filter. A polarizing filter will eliminate a lot of the glare on the rocks in the waterfall, creating a more attractive picture. A warming filter will eliminate the bluish tint that water can take in lower light conditions.

Avoid taking shots of very low volume waterfalls or shots with a great deal of surrounding terrain. They will usually result in photographs in which the waterfall is overshadowed by the surrounding terrain. In general, it is a good idea to take a picture if you can fill at least 30% of the frame with water.

Some of the best waterfall photographs come from angles not directly in front of the waterfall. Side angles and diagonal angles can create depth in photos that cannot be obtained from "straight-ahead" photos of the front.

Last but not least, be careful while positioning yourself to take a photograph. No picture is worth falling off a cliff, spraining your ankle or ruining your film or equipment with an accidental dunking.

How to Use This Guide

The waterfalls in this guide are organized by region, from the western part of Massachusetts to the east. The westernmost regions, the Berkshires and the Connecticut River Valley, are the most mountainous and therefore the most likely to provide the steep elevations necessary for waterfalls. There are, however, several waterfalls worth visiting in central Massachusetts and the Boston area. At the beginning of each regional section in this guide there is a map showing the locations of all waterfalls listed (See *facing page*). The numbered waterfalls are arranged consecutively in groups so that the reader might more easily plan trips to visit several falls that are near to each other.

Within its region, each waterfall is listed by name, along with the town in which it is found. In the case of many of the falls, the location within a State Forest or Reservation is also listed. Each waterfall listing shows walking distance, walking time, and difficulty (rating), as well as the USGS topographical map(s) covering the walk. Each listing also includes driving directions to the falls, trail notes, and a photo of the waterfall destination.

The name listed for each waterfall is either the actual (official or geographic) name of the fall, or the name of the brook or stream (when no official name exists), or the name of some lake or other nearby feature (when no name exists for the brook or stream).

All the distances listed in this book are approximate. The estimated walking times are for healthy adults and are *one-way* only, unless otherwise specified.

Once you have decided on which waterfall(s) to visit, it is highly recommended that you read through the directions and trail notes *completely* prior to embarking on your waterfall trip. This will give you clues as to what kind of terrain to expect (and thus, appropriate shoes or clothing to wear), how long it will take (and thus, how much water or food to bring), whether to bring insect repellant, etc.

The Berkshire Region

1. Bash Bish Falls
2. Sage's Ravine Brook
3. Bear Rock Falls
4. Race Brook
5. Umpachene Falls
6. Campbell Falls
7. Marguerite Falls
8. Otis Reservoir
9. Monument Mountain
10. Wahconah Falls
11. Windsor Jambs
12. Ross/Tannery Brooks
13. Twin Cascades
14. Bellevue Falls
15. Peck Brook – Lower Falls
16. Peck Brook – Upper Falls
17. Deer Hill Falls
18. Money Brook
19. March Cataract Falls
20. The Cascade
21. Hudson Brook Chasm

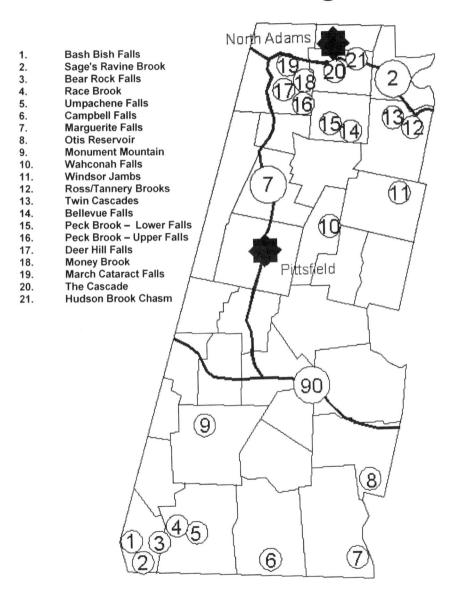

Bash Bish Falls

1

Bash Bish Falls

Bash Bish Falls State Park
Mount Washington State Forest
Mount Washington, MA
Distance: 0.2 to 0.5 mile
Walking Time: 5 to 20 minutes
Rating: Moderate to Challenging (steep sections)
USGS Map: Ashley Falls

Directions:

From Routes 23 and 41 in Egremont, go south on Route 41 around Mill Pond and take a right onto Mount Washington Road. Go south for 5.1 miles (at the town line this road becomes East Street), and turn right onto Hatch Hill Road, an unmarked dirt road. After only 0.25 mile, turn left onto West Street, another unmarked dirt road. After about 1.5 miles, Bash Bish Falls Road is on the right. Park at the first lot on the left for a short, steep walk, or go further on down the road to the second parking lot for 0.5 mile of easy walking.

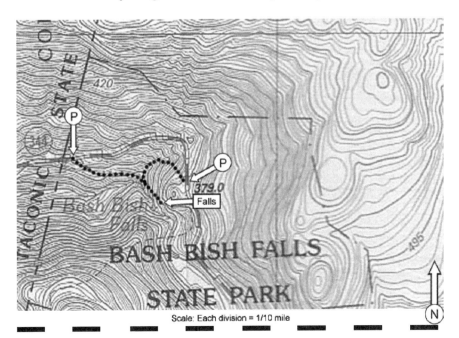

Scale: Each division = 1/10 mile

Trail Notes:

You can hear the falls from the upper lot. There is a viewing area above the gorge. You can see out into New York, and a bit of the other side of the gorge, but you won't see the falls from here. The trail down is steep, in some places with stone stairs or wooden water bars cut in. You'll pass over a log bridge before bearing left and down steeply toward the sound of the falls.

The falls are split, with the upper and lower falls totaling 80 feet. The upper fall is really a series of smaller falls or cascades, flowing through a 1000-foot gorge. The lower fall, pictured here, is approximately 50 feet, with a tremendous amount of water flowing in the spring. This fall is split again, roaring around both sides of a massive spur, at the chokepoint of the gorge.

The trail continues across the stream on some huge boulders, and if the water is low enough to cross, you should take the steep trail up to the top of the gorge. It isn't very wide, maybe 100-200 yards across, but it's a very long way down! There are some excellent vantages off this trail. You can re-cross the stream upstream of the gorge and return to the road by the upper parking lot.

BASH BISH FALLS CAN BE VERY DANGEROUS

The following regulations have been established for the area around the Falls:

1. Swimming is not allowed above or below the Falls.
2. Drinking is prohibited.
3. Camping is not allowed.
4. Climbing is allowed by permit only (contact the Park Supervisor - see below)
5. All pets must be leashed.
6. The Falls area is open from dawn to dusk.

Mount Washington State Forest

Bash Bish Falls is part of the 4500 acres of Mount Washington State Forest, managed by the Dept. of Conservation and Recreation, Division of Forests and Parks. This rugged, mountainous area offers various recreational opportunities and scenic vistas. Backpack camping is available year round at tent sites located approximately two miles from the park headquarters on East Street. Hikers can find roughly 30 miles of trails in the forest, including the ridge-top South Taconic Trail with stunning views of Massachusetts, New York and Connecticut. Also nearby is the Appalachian Trail. Hunting and fishing are popular here, with trout found in both the ponds and streams of the forest. In the winter, 21 miles of trail are open to skiing and snowmobiling. For further information, contact: Park Supervisor, Mt. Washington State Forest

RFD 3   Mt. Washington, MA 01258   413-528-0330

Geology and History of the Falls

Touted as "the state's most dramatic waterfall", the waters of Bash Bish Falls begin at a spring high in Mount Washington. The river falls through a steep set of cascades leading up to the actual falls which are composed of two powerful cascades around a large boulder and into a deep pool. The left stream actually changes direction about halfway down. Beyond the pool, the river continues on through a gorge with several lower cascades. After the 200-foot plunge of the Falls, Bash Bish Brook continues on a gentler course into New York State until it finally joins the Hudson River on its way to the Atlantic.

Waterfalls are short lived, "unimportant" geologic phenomenon when compared with events like the formation of mountain ranges. Bash Bish Brook, like all other streambeds in New England, is only as old as the retreat of the last glacier that covered the region about 11,000 years ago. During the melting of the last glacier, mounds of glacial debris blocked streambeds. When dammed streams finally broke through, they cascaded wildly down mountains, often following joints or weaknesses in the structure of the mountain and creating waterfalls.

A white quartz dike, which angles across the gorge halfway up the falls, is the result of hot silica-rich liquid escaping from within the earth 400 million years ago. The liquid forced itself upwards along a weakness in the gorge. The water of the brook has cut away enough rock to make this seam visible.

Jean Roemer, a college professor, became enchanted with Bash Bish Falls in the early part of the 19th century. He bought the Falls in 1860, and nearby he built an elaborate Swiss-style chalet mansion which eventually burned down. Roemer invited Charles Blondin (the French acrobat who had walked across Niagara Falls on a tightrope in 1858) to come to Bash Bish. Blondin placed a rope across the gorge and easily crossed it. However, he supposedly found Bash Bish more frightening than Niagara because of the black boulder-lined chasm beneath him.

In 1924, the Massachausetts Department of Conservation (now called the Department of Conservation and Recreation) recognized the area's scenic value and purchased 400 acres surrounding Bash Bish Falls. During the 1960s, the state obtained 4,000 more acres, and named the entire area Mount Washington State Forest.

Unfortunately, the Falls have a history of tragic events. Inexperienced climbers have fallen to their deaths when crumbly ledges gave way. Careless swimmers have plunged into pools without realizing rocks lay near the surface. During the 1960s, two or three people died in accidents each year. Accidents have been reduced since 1973, when a steel and cable fence was built, and State rangers began frequent patrolling.

Sage's Ravine Brook

2
Sage's Ravine Brook

Mount Washington State Forest area
Mount Washington, MA
Distance: 1.5 miles
Walking Time: 45 minutes
USGS Map: Ashley Falls
Rating: Moderate to Challenging

Directions:

From Routes 23 and 41 in Egremont, go south on Route 41 around Mill Pond and take a right onto Mount Washington Road. Go south for 5.1 miles (at the town line this road becomes East Street) and turn right onto Hatch Hill Road, an unmarked dirt road. After only 0.25 mile, turn left onto West Street, another unmarked dirt road. After 1.5 miles, you'll pass the turn to Bash Bish Falls. Continue on West Street for another mile, staying right at the intersection with Cross Road. Another mile brings you back to East Street. Bear right and follow East Street another 2.7 miles to parking at a gate just past a granite marker at the Connecticut state line.

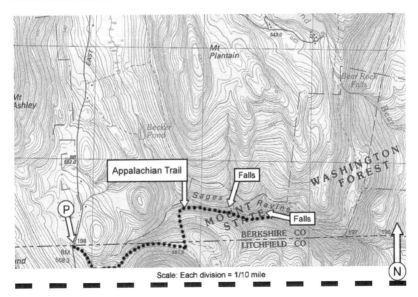

Trail Notes:

Go past the gate onto land owned by the Appalachian Mountain Club, taking a wide, unmarked trail. The going here is easy; you're walking a flat trail through the hardwoods with a stream bubbling off to your left, and you can make very good time. Soon, you will pass an AMC shelter off to your right. Cross over the stream entering from your right on a log bridge, and start descending. Soon you'll pass over a smaller stream on another log bridge.

In about 0.75 mile you'll intersect the white-blazed Appalachian Trail (AT). Look around here and note the log bridge and stepping stones, because there is no sign, and you don't want to miss this turn on the way back. Go left (north) on the AT, and you'll soon come to a junction with Paradise Trail, which heads off to Route 41 to the right. Continue left on the AT, and in 0.25 mile you'll reach the upper end of the ravine.

As you walk the 0.5 mile of the ravine on the left bank, you'll pass several streams coming into Sage's Ravine Brook from left and right, some with little falls of their own. Note the small fall dropping into Sage's Ravine Brook from the left, seeming to land on top of the boulder. Sage's Ravine Brook has several cascades, from a few feet to 20 feet. There is almost no sun down here, and it's much cooler, although in mosquito season it could be brutal.

Geology and History of the Falls

Sage's Ravine is a valley carved by Sage's Ravine Brook; it passes through a forest of hemlock, maple, ash and oak on the border of Connecticut. The Connecticut Department of Environmental Protection owns the Connecticut portion, and the Massachusetts portion is protected by the National Park Service, because the Appalachian Trail runs along part of the Ravine. In some places, easily dissolved limestone lies under the ravine, and consequently the stream disappears underground into subterranean water passages, only to shoot up again further downstream. The headwaters of Sage's Ravine Brook are protected in the Mount Plantain Preserve to the north.

The brook and the ravine were named after Zachias Sage, a revolutionary war veteran who is buried at Candee-Sage's Cemetery, which is located 0.25 mile north of Sage's Ravine. "Sage's Mill," a forge powered by the brook, used to be located at the junction of Route 41 and Sage's Brook, an area that was formerly known as Joyceville, on the Massachusetts/Connecticut state line.

3

Bear Rock Falls

Mount Washington State Forest area
Mount Washington, MA
Distance: 3 miles
Walking Time: 2 hours
USGS Map: Ashley Falls
Rating: Moderate to Challenging

Directions:

From Routes 23 and 41 in Egremont, go south on Route 41 around Mill Pond and take a right onto Mount Washington Road. Go south for 5.1 miles (at the town line this road becomes East St.) and turn right onto Hatch Hill Road, an unmarked dirt road. After only 0.25 mile, turn left onto West Street, another unmarked dirt road. After 1.5 miles, you'll pass the turn to Bash Bish Falls. Continue on West Street for one mile, staying right at the intersection with Cross Road. Another mile brings you back to East Street. Bear right and follow East Street for 2.7 miles to parking at a gate just past a granite marker at the Connecticut state line.

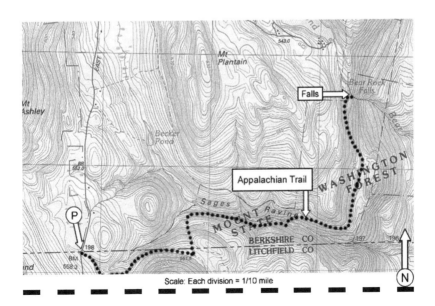

Bear Rock Falls

Trail Notes:

First, you follow the trail notes for Sage's Ravine Brook. Go past the gate onto land owned by the Appalachian Mountain Club, taking a wide, unmarked trail. The going here is easy; you're walking a flat trail through the hardwoods with a stream bubbling off to your left, and you can make very good time. Soon, you will pass an AMC shelter off to your right. Cross over the stream entering from your right on a log bridge, and start descending. Soon you'll pass over a smaller stream on another log bridge.

In about 0.75 mile you'll intersect the Appalachian Trail (AT). Look around here and note the log bridge and stepping stones, because there is no sign, and you don't want to miss this turn on the way back. Go left (north) on the AT, and you'll soon come to a junction with Paradise Trail, which heads off to Route 41 to the right. Continue left on the AT, and in 0.25 mile you'll reach the upper end of the ravine.

As you walk the 0.5 mile of the ravine on the left bank, you'll pass several streams coming into Sage's Ravine Brook from left and right, some with little falls of their own. Note the small fall dropping into Sage's Ravine Brook from the left, seeming to land on top of the boulder.

After you have followed the above directions to Sage's Ravine, you now follow these directions to Bear Rock Falls:
At the sign indicating the end of the ravine, cross the brook on some boulders and continue along the Appalachian Trail north, going sharply uphill. You'll hear the falls below, as you climb up out of the ravine, until you turn away at the top of the hill and enter an easier stretch through the hardwoods.

The trail is mostly easy walking, with a few short climbs. Soon after one climb, you'll cross a small stream, and you'll come to Laurel Ridge camping area off to the left, with (at the time of this writing) a sign indicating that Bear Rock camping area is closed for re-vegetation. In only a few feet you'll find a trail heading right, through the old Bear Rock camping area, now unused, and heading toward Bear Rock Brook and the head of the falls.

The falls are listed as 90 to 100 feet high, but they seem to be much higher. They are hard to see from the top, and in fact you won't be able to see the bottom of the falls through the trees. You'll need to be very careful if you venture down the very steep cliffs to the bottom of the falls.

Race Brook- Upper Falls

4

Race Brook - Upper Falls

Mount Everett State Reservation vicinity
Sheffield, MA
Distance: 0.75 mile
Walking Time: 30 minutes
USGS Map: Ashley Falls
Rating: Challenging

Directions:

From the junction of Routes 23 and 41 in Egremont, take a left at Mill Pond, going south on Route 41. After 5 miles is a small public parking area on the right.

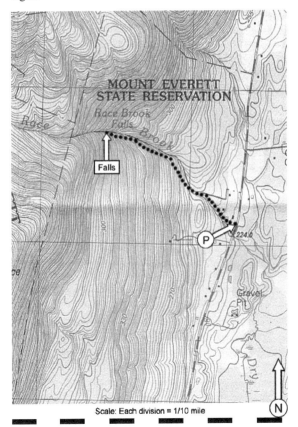

Scale: Each division = 1/10 mile

Trail Notes:

Take the blue-triangle-marked trail exiting the parking area to the left, beyond the sign. The trail crosses a small stream, and then skirts counter clockwise around the outside of a nice field with tall grass and wildflowers. You'll soon enter the pine woods, and begin a climb. After about 0.25 mile you'll turn left at a sign indicating the Appalachian Trail 2 miles via falls.

The trail becomes narrow at this point, with mountain laurel crowding in on either side. You'll break out of the laurel just above Race Brook. Go upstream a short way to a crossing, where you'll put the brook on your right. At high water periods, this crossing can be difficult, and you may need a hiking stick to give you extra support when you're reaching for the next rock.

After you cross the brook, the trail swings around clockwise, climbing higher and higher from the brook. Soon you'll come to a sign indicating Race Brook Trail Campsite / Lower Falls Loop Trail. Bear left here and begin to climb more sharply uphill away from the sound of the brook.

Soon you will switchback to the right, back toward the brook. When you come back to the brook, look over the edge and you'll see two or three more falls above the second lower fall. If you wish to see them, you will find a faint red-marked trail leading away downstream from just below the upper fall. The trail crosses the brook at the base of the upper fall on its way to the junction with the Appalachian Trail another mile and a quarter up. From there you can go north to the summit of Mount Everett, or south to the summit of Mount Race.

This upper fall is around 80 feet in two giant steps, with an excellent volume of water. The fall looks like it's trying to undercut a nearly vertical ledge on the left running nearly perpendicular to the brook, forcing the brook to bear left and toward you.

Please note: All pets must be leashed.

What's Underneath a Waterfall

One way to categorize waterfalls is by the bedrock structure that formed them. For example, streams flowing over granite with evenly spaced cracks (called joints) tend to pluck out blocks of rock, creating steplike falls. Many falls occur where a stream crosses a resistant rock called slate.

Race Brook - Lower Falls

Mount Everett State Reservation vicinity
Sheffield, MA
Distance: 0.5 mile
Walking Time: 20 minutes
USGS Map: Ashley Falls
Rating: Moderate

Directions:

From the junction of Routes 23 and 41 in Egremont, take a left at Mill Pond, going south on Route 41. After 5 miles is a small parking area on the right.

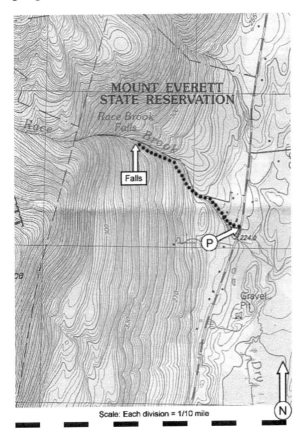

Race Brook- Lower Falls

Trail Notes:

Take the blue-triangle-marked trail exiting the parking area to the left, beyond the sign. The trail crosses a small stream, and then skirts counter clockwise around the outside of a nice field with tall grass and wildflowers. You'll soon enter the pine woods, and begin a climb. After about 0.25 mile you'll turn left at a sign indicating the Appalachian Trail 2 miles via falls.

The trail becomes narrow at this point, with mountain laurel crowding in on either side. You'll break out of the laurel just above Race Brook. Go upstream a short way to a crossing, where you'll put the brook on your right. At high water periods, this crossing can be difficult, and you may need a hiking stick to give you extra support when you're reaching for the next rock.

After you cross the brook, the trail swings around clockwise, climbing higher and higher from the brook. Soon you'll come to a sign indicating Race Brook Trail Campsite / Lower Falls Loop Trail, and you'll bear right here onto a less-used side trail marked in faded blue, leading down into the gully to the right to the lower falls. After nearly a half mile from the parking area, you'll come to a fork at a sign indicating Falls View, with an arrow pointing in either direction. To the right, in 100 yards you'll curl around counter clockwise and find the lowest fall, pictured here.

This fall is huge, easily 50 feet. It drops in two steps, with the upper entering in from the left, then abruptly turning right and plunging toward you before dropping straight about 30 or 35 feet, and tumbling another 15 feet to left and right below.

Return to the sign and follow it going up (to the left if you had just come upon it from the main trail) to the head of the lower fall where you have an awesome view out to the east. Just 100 feet upstream is the next fall, another impressive one. This fall appears to be only a few feet wide at the top and tumbles down once or twice, about 8 feet in height, and then drops left to right another 20 feet, fanning out to 12 feet wide, to fall into a pool below.

Note: All pets must be leashed.

5

Umpachene Falls

New Marlborough, MA
Distance: Roadside
Walking Time: --
USGS Map: Ashley Falls
Rating: Easy

Directions:

From Route 57 in the center of New Marlborough, immediately in front of the big white church, go south on New Marlborough / Southfield Road. After 1.2 miles, and just before the bridge, take a right onto Southfield Road. After 0.1 mile, turn left onto Mill River Road. Follow Mill River Road for about 0.75 mile, and take a right onto Hasdell Street just before the bridge. Go 0.4 mile and you will find parking on the left.

Trail Notes:

The falls are at the far end of a little park. The park is open to the public. The road is not plowed in the winter, but you can hike in or snowshoe to the falls. The park is open Memorial Day to Labor Day. There are picnic tables, grills, a play area with swings, and benches along the river. The park itself is located in the V created at the confluence of the Umpachene and Konkapot Rivers, with the Umpachene on your left. Just past the swings and the remains of a building, the Umpachene Falls drop some thirty feet in three steps – the upper two in sheer drops, and the lower in a cascade. Swimming is allowed.

Campbell Falls

6

Campbell Falls

Campbell Falls State Park
New Marlborough, MA
Distance: 0.1 mile
Walking Time: 5 minutes
USGS Map: Tolland Center
Rating: Easy

Directions:

From Route 57 in the center of New Marlborough, go south onto New Marlborough / Southfield Road. After 1.3 miles, bear left onto Norfolk Road. Continue on Norfolk Road for 4.4 miles (almost to the border of Massachusett and Connecticut), and take a right onto Campbell Falls Road. Parking is on the left in 0.3 mile.

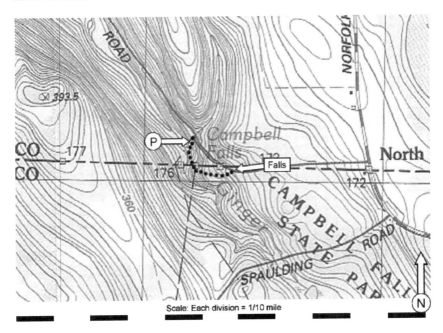

Scale: Each division = 1/10 mile

Trail Notes:

You will park just over the line into Connecticut. Take the short trail out the back of the lot, past the sign. You will go fairly steeply downhill, bearing to the right, on a white-marked trail. You will hear the falls as soon as you exit your car, and soon you will hear Ginger Creek on your left, which enters Whiting River just below the falls.

After only 100 yards, just beyond a stone marker indicating the Massachusetts / Connecticut border, you'll cross back into Massachusetts and reach the base of the falls. The falls are situated in a small gorge or ravine, and fall 60 feet in two steps, with the upper dropping 35 or 40 feet straight down, and the lower section splitting around a boulder.

There are trails to the top of the falls which branch off the main trail down to the base of the falls, or you can continue on Campbell Falls Road a bit further to a second parking area at the head of the falls.

There is a very large volume of water here, with a nice pool at the base of the fall. The falls seem to have eroded into a cliff or ledge on the left, with the river making a turn to the right, from the initial drop, and back to the left after the pool. Between the two falls there is a boulder in the center of the stream, upon which you can perch for a good view of the upper fall, but there is a lot of mist here. Be careful jumping here as the mist may make the stone treacherous.

Note: No fires or camping. The area is closed at sunset.

Why Does the Water Look Dirty?

The water of many streams may have a dark orange or brown color, but usually this is not because of dangerous man-made pollution. It is due to the tannin from dissolved plant matter, often from wetlands that drain into the brook.

Likewise, the white foamy accumulations that you may see are not from soapy pollution, but are also the result of organic compounds in the water.

7

Marguerite Falls

New Boston / Sandisfield, MA
Distance: Roadside
Walking Time: --
USGS Map: Tolland Center
Rating: Easy

Directions:

From the junction of Routes 57 and 8 in New Boston (a village in Sandisfield), follow Route 8 south for 3.6 miles to a rest area on the left side of the road.

Trail Notes:

Walk back up Route 8 north for 150 feet to the bridge over the falls. You can take the trail just before the bridge on the right, to view the falls in the shade of the bridge, but you'll miss the upper section. The best view is from the bridge on the left.

These falls are on the unnamed brook flowing from Lake Marguerite. It's a short brook, soon spilling into the Colebrook River Lake, but before doing so it makes a beautiful fall as it passes under Route 8.

The falls are about 50 feet, cascading down the ledge in two sections. The upper section drops around 15 feet, but can only be seen from the bridge above. The lower section is about 30 feet high, splitting around a raised section about half way down, where a few trees and some brush are growing.

There is a nice volume of water flowing. You can see the lower section from under the bridge, crossing on the large boulders scattered about. The rocks of the streambed are worn smooth, and you'll need to be careful walking here.

8

Otis Reservoir

Tolland State Forest
Otis, MA
Distance: Roadside
Walking Time: --
USGS Map: Otis
Rating: Easy

Directions:

From the Otis / Blandford town line, follow Route 23 west for 1 mile to West
Shore Road on your left. Follow West Shore Road for 0.7 mile to Tolland Road
on the left. Follow Tolland Road for 0.8 mile to a small dirt parking area on
either side of the road, just before the dam, each large enough for two cars.
*Follow the signs for Tolland State Forest.

Trail Notes:

Take the foot trail leading into the woods across the road from the reservoir, and
enter a mixed forest on a wide trail. At a junction just a few feet into the woods,
bear right and start to descend.

After only 25 feet, take a left onto a side trail heading down the gorge toward
the sound of water. When you get to the bottom of the gorge, turn left and walk
along the mossy boulders upstream a bit to a 25-foot fall on the overflow brook,
dropping cleanly over the ledges bordering the amphitheatre-shaped gorge.
There isn't a large flow in the summer, so try to time your visit for the spring.

Return to where you reached the streambed and go downstream for a few feet to
find where Fall River enters from the left, dropping down a 35-foot fall in three
sections. The uppermost section, glimpsed through the trees, drops about 10 feet
and then drops again for a tumble or two in a cascade, before splitting into four
streamlets over a huge piece of boulder / ledge.

For photo of Otis Reservoir -- see page 163

9

Monument Mountain

Trustees of Reservations
Monument Mountain Reservation
Great Barrington, MA
Distance: 0.5 mile
Walking Time: 20 minutes
USGS Map: Great Barrington
Rating: Moderate

Directions:

Go south on Route 7 from the center of Stockbridge for 3 miles to the parking area for Monument Mountain on the right.

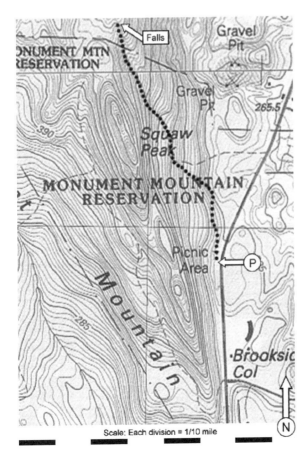

Scale: Each division = 1/10 mile

Falls at Monument Mountain

Trail Notes:

Follow the trail out the north end of the parking lot through the pines. The trail, marked with white dots, drops down into the hardwoods for a minute and then back into mixed forest and begins to climb. After 10 minutes you'll pass a large glacial erratic at the edge of the rubble field at the base of the ledges that signal the end of the first climb. You now pass through mountain laurel in a flat area. Soon you'll turn left and climb again, passing near a small stream with a chute, almost like it could be a water slide. A hundred yards past the log bridge brings you to the fall. The fall drops some 30 feet, the first 20 feet rolling and fanning over a huge boulder, and the last 10 feet falling into a small pool. There is a small cave tucked behind and to the side of the fall.

While you're here, you might consider following the rest of the loop to the summit. Monument Mountain, a Trustees of Reservations property, affords a beautiful walk.

Monument Mountain Reservation

The mountain is 1,735 feet at its peak, overlooking the hills and valleys of southern Berkshire County. Three miles of trails lead through the canopy forest of white pine and oaks with tulip trees, maples, chestnut saplings and mountain laurel. Rock outcrops hide small caves and several streams wind through the forest. The Reservation is open daily, year-round.

For almost two centuries, Monument Mountain has been a source of inspiration to poets, novelists, and painters. During William Cullen Bryant's stay in Great Barrington (1815-1825), he penned "Monument Mountain," a lyrical poem that tells the story of a Mohican maiden whose forbidden love for her cousin led her to leap to her death from the mountain's cliffs. A rock cairn marks the spot where she is buried, giving the mountain its name, Mountain of the Monument. On August 5, 1850, Nathaniel Hawthorne and Herman Melville enjoyed a well-chronicled picnic hike up Monument Mountain. A thunderstorm forced them to seek refuge in a cave where a lengthy and vigorous discussion ensued, inspiring powerful ideas for Melville's new book, *Moby Dick*.

The Trustees of Reservations is dedicated to preserving properties of exceptional scenic, historic and ecological value throughout the state. This non-profit conservation organization relies for support entirely upon membership dues, admission fees and voluntary contributions. For more information, contact:

The Trustees of Reservations
Western Regional Office, The Mission House
P.O. Box 792, Sergeant Street, Stockbridge, MA 01262
(413) 298-3239   *www.thetrustees.org*

10
Wahconah Falls

Wahconah Falls State Park
Dalton, MA
Distance: 0.1 mile
Walking Time: 5 minutes
USGS Map: Pittsfield East
Rating: Easy

Directions:

From the middle of Pittsfield, MA, take Route 9 East for 7.1 miles. At the sign to Wahconah Falls State Park, turn onto North Road and then immediately onto a dirt road (Wahconah Falls Road). The dirt road is rutted but passable by regular vehicles. The parking lot then comes up after 0.5 mile on your right.

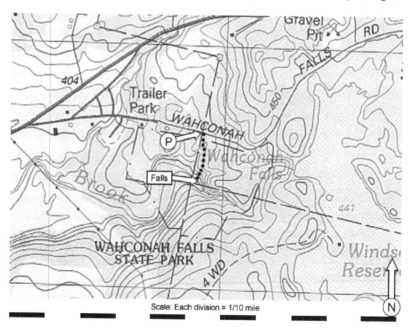

Scale: Each division = 1/10 mile

Wahconah Falls

Trail Notes:

Go past the gates at the rear of the parking lot onto a short trail through the hemlocks. Soon you will go through a small picnic area with tables and charcoal grills. The trail continues on to the falls, which measure 40 feet.

Waterpower

The flow of water out of a six-inch pipe and directed onto a small waterwheel is capable of producing between 2 and 5 horsepower. In the days of water-powered mills, this amount of waterpower was enough to turn a lathe and operate a bellows, a fulling mill, a small carding machine, or a small machine for making shoe pegs. Many such small operations were set up along streams in Massachusetts and were called shops. These, along with grist mills and saw mills, took advantage of this natural power resource.

47

11
Windsor Jambs

Windsor Jambs State Park, Windsor State Forest
Windsor, MA
Distance: 0.1mile
Walking Time: 5 minutes
USGS Map: Ashfield
Rating: Easy

Directions:

From the Cummington / Windsor town line, go 0.5 mile east on Route 9 to a left onto West Main St. After only 0.1 mile, go left onto River Road. After 2.9 miles turn right, off the pavement, onto Lower Road. After 0.25 mile, you go straight through the 4-way intersection with Windigo Road, and after 0.2 mile, turn right onto Schoolhouse Road. Parking is only 100 feet ahead on the right in a dirt lot with an iron gate but no sign.

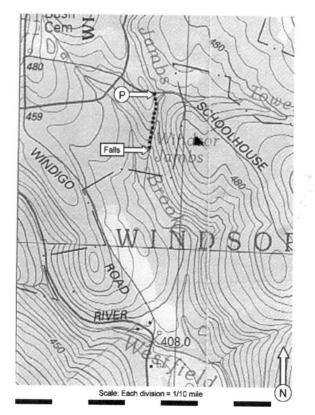

Scale: Each division = 1/10 mile

Windsor Jambs

Trail Notes:

The trail is out at the far end of the parking lot, but you'll hear the falls as soon as you step out of the car. There is a fence along the gorge to keep people from venturing too close, but it doesn't help when you're trying to get a good photo of the falls!

You'll first see two falls back to back, at the head of the jambs. Each is fairly short, but with a large flow. The first splits around a spur of rock, then comes together at the pool before immediately splitting around a second spur and flowing into the jambs. Walking along the fence, you'll see some other nice falls, and you can get fair pictures of them from above, but you won't find a spot to get the whole vista on film. Don't let this discourage you because it's a nice trip, and an easy walk for all but the youngest children, and you can get some interesting photos.

Ross Brook

12
Ross Brook / Tannery Brook

Savoy Mountain State Forest
Savoy, MA
Distance: 0.25 mile
Walking Time: 10 minutes
USGS Map: Cheshire
Rating: Moderate

Directions:

From Charlemont, take Route 2 west to Black Brook Road, a left turn located 1.5 miles past the Charlemont / Savoy line on a sharp curve. Continue on Black Brook Road for 1.4 miles to Tannery Road on the right. Follow along this dirt road for 0.7 mile to a parking area just past a small pond on the left.

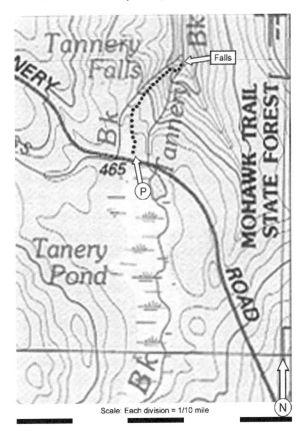

Scale: Each division = 1/10 mile

Trail Notes:

Follow the blue-triangle-marked trail out the rear of the parking area past the sign, and enter the pines. The trail begins to descend quickly, with Tannery Brook off to your right. Soon you'll hear Ross Brook to your left, and at this point you're walking downwards along a ridge between the two brooks. After only a few hundred yards, you'll descend some wooden stairs, and now follow along Ross Brook. You'll come right up to the brook at a bend, where the brook swings round and cascades down a small slope. There are cables strung along the edge for safety, and at this point you can look downstream and begin to see where the brook has eroded its way down into the ledge. The ledge here has split apart, with the right bank of the brook (where you're walking) pulling away downhill and forming a crack that the brook has filled and begun to undercut. At one point you are standing on ledge, with the brook running right under you.

The trail brings you to the head of the falls in another hundred yards or so. There are cables strung up here also. You can lean over and see the falls, but then continue along sharply to the right, taking a series of switchbacks down some wooden stairs. Be careful; there may be loose stairs. At the end of the first switchback you can see Tannery Brook entering from the right, and Ross Brook on the left. From here, the following directions will take you to either falls.

To Ross Brook Falls:

Continue down the stairs, and bear left along Tannery Brook. Go down the massive stone stairs to the large pool below the falls, just above the confluence of Ross and Tannery Brooks. The fall is tall, but does not have a tremendous flow. The upper section rolls over a long sloping ledge, with only a small drop to a small pool about 30 feet from the top. The brook then falls another 25 feet to drop into a smaller shelf, before dropping the final 12 feet into the pool before you.

To Tannery Brook Falls:

After you get off the last stair, bear right and go upstream a few feet to the base of the small pool below the falls. The falls are situated in a crack in the ledge. The ledge is jutting up vertically, and at some previous time, the ledge on the right bank slid somewhat downhill, opening the gap before you, which the brook has undercut and eroded.

Tannery Falls drops in a series of steps, with the first drop or two falling 6 or 8 feet each, and the last drop falling around 12 feet into a small pool. The flow isn't very large, but it is situated nicely with the ledges on either side.

Tannery Brook

Twin Cascades

13
Twin Cascades

Florida, MA
Distance: 0.25 mile
Walking Time: 15 minutes
USGS Map: North Adams
Rating: Easy to Moderate

Directions:

From the Mohawk Park on Route 2 in Charlemont, go east over the bridge, and take the first left onto Zoar Road. After 2.5 miles, take a left onto River Road. Follow River Road for 4.5 miles, and park near the railroad tracks.

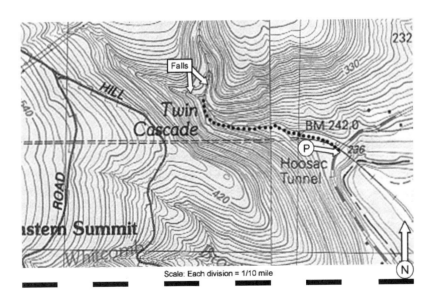

Scale: Each division = 1/10 mile

Trail Notes:

Follow the stream beside the entrance to the Hoosac Tunnel. Skirt past the remains of a dam and spillway, and hop down the far side on a log section cut out of a deadfall. Soon you will see little cascades. About 100 yards past the tunnel, just after you lose sight of the tracks behind you, the trail begins to fade. Watch for the trail to leave the stream and begin to climb away to your left. As you climb, the trail becomes more distinct, but you will see more deadfalls and other storm damage, requiring you to duck and scramble in some places.

After 0.25 mile, you will see a pair of cascades falling from left and right. They fall 50 and 80 feet into a common pool, and then fall again as one combined waterfall. The stream on the right is Cascade Brook, but there is no name shown on maps for the stream on the left (the taller of the two).

There is a huge flow here, and the mist is thick right below the common falls. In order to view the falls on the left, you will need to cross the stream or go up the dam. The dam appears to be natural, with some assistance given years ago by the railroad. There are large bolts jutting from the stone, as well as pipes and pieces of railroad track.

Note:

In May 2003, there were "No Trespassing" signs at the parking lot to the left of the road, on the Hoosac Tunnel side. The main purpose here is to keep people from loitering in the parking lot and to keep them from entering the tunnel. It is possible to park on the river side of the road in a lot designated for fishing. It is evidently customary for people to ignore the signs and go up the trail to the falls.

Caution:

Do not walk in or near the tunnel! These railroad tracks are actively in use.

14
Bellevue Falls

Adams, MA
Distance: Roadside
Walking Time: --
USGS Map: Cheshire
Rating: Easy

Directions:

From the junction of Routes 8 and 116 in the center of Adams, go south on Route 8 for 0.7 mile to Leonard Street on your left. Follow Leonard Street for 0.2 mile, and turn right onto Bellevue Avenue. After 0.1 mile on Bellevue Avenue, you'll enter Bellevue Cemetery. There are roads criss-crossing the cemetery, so to make it simple, take every right hand turn. You'll park at a tiny dirt parking area beside a section of split rail fence.

Trail Notes:

Follow the short trail out the left end of the parking area, past the fence. You'll dip into the pines, and after 100 feet you'll be at Dry Brook. The falls are about 6 or 8 feet high, cascading down a slippery slide of a ledge into a pool nearly 50 feet across. There are a ledges on either side of the falls, and many boulders upstream. Jumping from ledges is unsafe here and not recommended.

Bellevue Falls

15
Peck Brook- Lower Falls

Mount Greylock State Reservation vicinity
Adams, MA
Distance: 100 yards
Walking Time: --
USGS Map: Cheshire
Rating: Easy

Directions:

From Routes 2 & 8 in North Adams center, follow route 8 South for 4.6 miles to Friend Street on the right. Follow Friend Street for 1.5 miles to West Mountain Road on the right. Follow West Mountain Road for 0.2 mile and go 100 yards past the power lines and park on the right between white and orange gas pipelines on either side of the street. If you pass a large brown house on the left, you've gone too far.

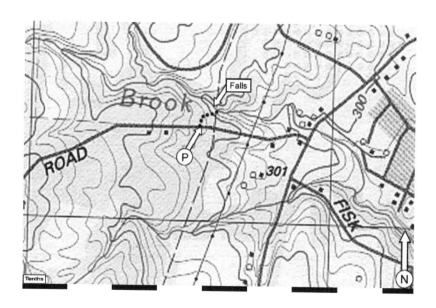

Peck Brook - Lower Falls

Trail Notes:

The trail heads off to the right just above the gas pipe and bears right and downhill. Continue along for 100 yards to the falls to your left. The falls have eroded down 40 feet through the stone, creating a small gorge from what must have been a great pothole at one time.

The first drop falls through a crack in the ledge, where the water has eaten into the ledge itself. The lower section breaks out at what appears to be the base of a split in this great pothole.

16
Peck Brook- Upper Falls

Mount Greylock State Reservation
Adams, MA
Distance: 1 Mile
Walking Time: 30 minutes
USGS Map: Cheshire
Rating: Moderate

Directions:

At the junction of Routes 2 and 7 in Williamstown, go south about 11.5 miles and take a left onto North Main Street in Lanesborough (sign for Mt. Greylock Visitor Center). Go 0.7 mile to a right onto Quarry Road, and another 0.4 mile to Rockwell Road on the left, passing the Visitor Center. Inside the Reservation, follow Rockwell Road for 7.8 miles to the junction with Notch Road on the left. Parking is across from Notch Road in a dirt lot.

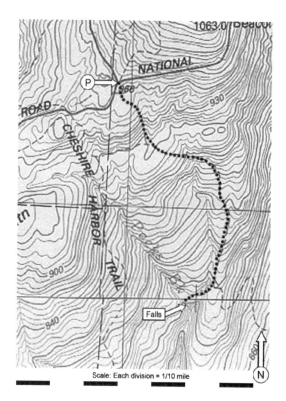

Scale: Each division = 1/10 mile

Peck Brook- Upper Falls

Trail Notes:

At the rear of the parking lot, follow the Gould Trail, heading through a mixed woods of short stunted trees. This trail is marked in blue rectangles. You'll head downhill fairly gently at first. Soon you'll enter a close, dark pine grove, and then you begin to descend more steeply. You'll go through a few switchbacks, and cross a few log bridges, before reaching a plank bridge after about 0.25 mile of walking. After the bridge, you'll pass an area with storm fencing on the right, where the hillside is fairly steep. After this section, the trail widens out more, and gets steeper yet. You'll bear left at a sign, where a faint trail or logging road heads off to the right.

After nearly a mile, you'll see a sign for Peck Brook Shelter, pointing you to the right. Follow this side trail a few hundred yards to the lean-to shelter facing Peck Brook. This is one of the few designated camping areas in the reservation. There is a fireplace here, and a little bit of a view peeking through the trees. Follow one of the faint trails down the very steep bank to the base of the falls, just 100 feet past the shelter. From the pool at the base of the falls, you can still see the corner of the shelter. The falls are about 25 feet, rolling down a chute or crack in the ledge, almost making a water slide. There is not a large flow of water here except in early spring.

After viewing the falls, you might like to drive to the nearby summit, only a few minutes away. Mount Greylock is the highest peak in Massachusetts.

The Sound Physics of Waterfalls

Waterfalls can pound the earth so hard that you can feel the vibration in the ground from a considerable distance. For most waterfalls, one frequency of vibration is dominant. The shorter the waterfall, the higher the frequency. Also, the product of the frequency and the height of the waterfall is always $1/4$ of the speed of sound in water.

Why should the frequency have anything to do with the height of the waterfall? The dominant frequency may result from an acoustic standing wave set up in the falling water column, much like a standing wave can be produced in a tube with one open end and one closed end.

Why should their product be one-fourth the speed of sound? The factor of one-fourth results from the speed of sound in water being one fourth that of air.

17

Deer Hill Falls

Mount Greylock State Reservation
Williamstown, MA
Distance: 0.5 mile
Walking Time: 20 minutes
USGS Map: North Adams
Rating: Moderate

Directions:

At the junction of Routes 2 and 7 in Williamstown, drive south for about 11.5 miles and take a left onto North Main Street in Landesborough (sign for Mt. Greylock Visitor Center). Go 0.7 mile to a right onto Quarry Road, and another 0.4 mile to Rockwell Road on the left, passing the Visitor Center. Follow Rockwell Road for 6.3 miles to Sperry Road on the left. At 0.6 mile further on, you can park at Sperry Campground. There may be a $2 parking fee (in season).

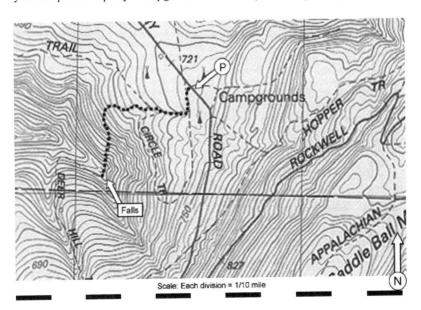

Scale: Each division = 1/10 mile

Deer Hill Falls

Trail Notes:

Go a few feet further down Sperry Road, and turn left into the camping area. Bear left, and continue through the campground toward the sound of the brook until you enter Deer Hill and Roaring Brook Trails. Almost immediately you'll cross a wooden bridge over Roaring Brook, and bear right.

You'll walk a well-defined trail through a mixed forest, marked with blue rectangles. All the trails on Mount Greylock are well maintained to prevent erosion of the trails, as well as the clearing of deadfalls. Soon the trail begins to descend a bit more steeply, as you walk with the brook on your right.

At about 0.2 mile you'll again cross over Roaring Brook and turn left, leaving Roaring Brook Trail and staying alongside the brook. The trail gets steeper yet, and a bit narrower. In 100 yards you'll veer to the right away from the stream. Here the trail gets more rocky, and some stone stairs have been cut into the soil. You'll take a switchback or two and begin to head back toward the brook.

Another hundred yards or more brings you to the falls. The falls are about 30 feet, fanning out from 12 feet wide at the top to nearly 25 feet wide at the base. There isn't a huge flow here, although it roars in the spring. The falls are more misty, giving the area at the base a kind of rain forest feel. The fall is shower-like, with hundreds of little sprays, and the left side of the fall being the heaviest.

Pay attention when you leave. The trail hairpins at the base of the falls, and you want to be sure to take the right hand trail back to your car.

How much energy is produced by waterfalls?

A tremendous amount of energy is developed by the world's streams as they descend to the ocean. Imagine all the continental runoff concentrated in one gigantic waterfall. First, we can estimate that the total water available for runoff is about 8,000 cubic miles of water that courses off the land and into the sea every year. We can also state that on the average, the surface of the land stands about one-half mile above sea level. Thus, every year, about 8,000 cubic miles of water tumbles down our hypothetical waterfall that is one-half mile high. Such a waterfall could supply about 200 horsepower continuously for each square mile of land on the entire earth.

18

Money Brook

Mount Greylock State Reservation
Williamstown, MA
Distance: 0.75 mile
Walking Time: 40 minutes
USGS Map: North Adams
Rating: Moderate

Directions:

From the junction of Routes 2, 8, and 8A in the center of North Adams, follow Route 2 west for 1.3 miles to a left onto Notch Road. Follow Notch Road for 5 miles to a small parking area on the right.

If you're coming from Deer Hill Falls (# 17) or March Cataract Falls (# 19), come 3.9 miles down Notch Road from the summit area to this parking area (now on the left).

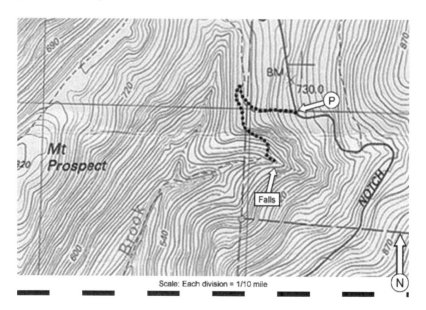

Scale: Each division = 1/10 mile

Money Brook

Trail Notes:

The trail leads downhill out the right side of the parking area. Travel downhill, fairly steeply, and after 0.3 mile you'll come to the junction with the Money Brook Trail. Take a left, and follow Money Brook Trail. Soon the trail starts descending a bit steeper and becoming narrow, with brush crowding the trail. Turn to the right, following down along the edge of a ravine, after a little vista. Continue along, going fairly steeply downhill and in just a few feet you'll turn sharply left and head down into the ravine. Nearly at the base of the ravine, bear left at the sign for Money Brook Falls. The falls are about 70 feet in height, dropping in a few steps, with the main, upper fall about 35 feet tall. A few cascades tumble below for 25 feet or more.

19

March Cataract Falls

Mount Greylock State Reservation
Williamstown, MA
Distance: 0.75 mile
Walking Time: 30 minutes
USGS Map: North Adams
Rating: Moderate

Directions:

At the junction of Routes 2 and 7 in Williamstown, drive south for about 11.5 miles and take a left onto North Main Street in Lanesborough (sign for Mt. Greylock Visitor Center). Go 0.7 mile to a right onto Quarry Road, and another 0.4 mile to Rockwell Road on the left, passing the Visitor Center. Follow Rockwell Road for 6.3 miles to Sperry Road on the left. At 0.6 mile further on, you can park at Sperry Campground. There may be a $2 parking fee (in season).

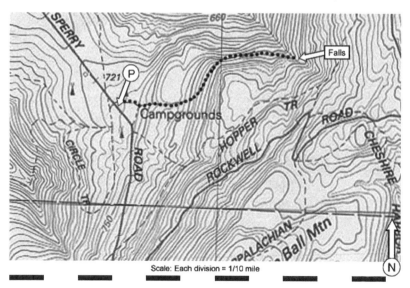

Scale: Each division = 1/10 mile

March Cataract Falls

Trail Notes:

From the parking area, continue down Sperry Road for a few feet to a right hand turn. Follow this short dirt road to the overflow parking at the corner, and take March Cataract Falls trail, which begins right at the corner. Immediately, you'll begin to climb along a wide stony trail marked with blue rectangles. Quite soon, you'll cross a small runoff stream and climb more steeply. Then the trail levels out and begins to follow along a level contour, becoming narrower.

After about 0.25 mile, the trail begins to descend, fairly steeply. You can catch glimpses of Stony Ledge across The Hopper. The Hopper is a glacial cirque, a huge valley cut into Mount Greylock by glaciers ages ago. March Cataract Falls is at the headwall of one of the side cuts leading into The Hopper. At this point you're heading toward the summit, but traveling downhill. After a few switchbacks, you'll cross a log bridge over a deep cut carved out by a runoff stream.

Just beyond the bridge, you'll come to March Cataract Falls. It's fairly open here, and the sun gets in, making it a great spot to take a break. The falls come in from the right and drop about 25 or 30 feet, fanning out along the way. The flow is not heavy except in the spring. Off to the left about 50 feet, you can see where the brook drops in a separate fall during spring runoff.

20
The Cascade

Cascade Park
North Adams, MA
Distance: 0.5 mile
Walking Time: 20 minutes
USGS Map: North Adams
Rating: Easy

Directions:

From the junction of Routes 2, 8, and 8A in the center of North Adams, follow Route 2 west for 1.2 miles to Marion Avenue on the left. Follow Marion Avenue for 0.3 mile, and park at the end of the road. There is a small area on the right with logs at the edge. Don't park in the fenced area where Marion Avenue comes to a dead-end in front of the last house on the street. Looking at the map, you might think that that it would be easier to come in from Reservoir Road, but that access is via private land.

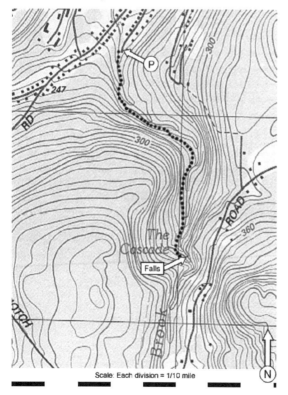

Scale: Each division = 1/10 mile

The Cascade

Trail Notes:

From the parking area, continue on to the end of the street and take the trail to the right of the fence. The trail is wide and flat -- easy walking for all ages. After only a hundred yards or so, you'll cross Notch brook on a small bridge, placing the stream on your left. Continue along, and soon the trail dips toward the stream. Perhaps the stream eroded the trail, but just follow along the right bank and in 20 or 30 feet the trail emerges from the streambed again. At this point you are about half way to the falls.

The remainder of the trail is relatively unremarkable. When you arrive at the falls, the trail climbs steeply, and if you want to get right to the base, you'll need to climb up the trail and cut down. You won't be able to get all the way to the base of the falls along the streambed. The falls are awesome, maybe 100 feet, and definitely not a cascade! They drop in two large steps, falling and fanning out beautifully, creating a loud roar.

21

Hudson Brook Chasm

Natural Bridge State Park
North Adams, MA
Distance: 0.2 mile
Walking Time: 15 minutes
USGS Map: North Adams
Rating: Easy

Directions:

From the junction of Routes 2 and 8, east of the center of North Adams, go north on Route 8 for 0.4 mile, following the signs for Natural Bridge State Park, and park on the left just beyond a large brick factory. There may be a $2 parking fee during the summer.

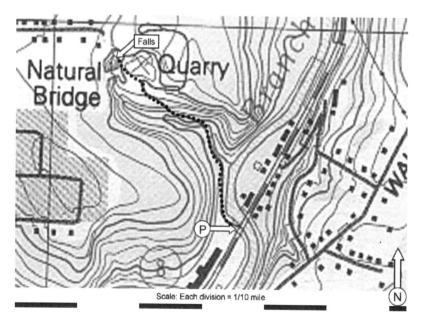

Scale: Each division = 1/10 mile

Hudson Brook Chasm

Trail Notes:

After a short walk along the bank of the polluted North Branch, you'll turn left along Hudson Brook. You can actually see the clear water of Hudson Brook briefly assault the green water of North Branch, before it is diluted and the pollution conquers in only a few feet.

Soon the road levels off and passes through an old marble quarry. (Please, no collecting is allowed.) Pass a large boulder, with a birch tree growing out the side of it, and climb the stairs to the left of the quarry to go over the chasm. Here you can see where Hudson Brook has worn its way through this large rock formation, and now flows through it some 30 or 40 feet below. Wooden stairs and walkways with railings allow you to view the evidence of water erosion, offering you great views, and taking you to the namesake natural bridge.

The natural bridge is where Hudson Brook wore its way right through the rock below, leaving a large bridge over one section of the brook. Further upstream you'll see a large dam built of the white marble quarried here, as well as the remains of a cement aqueduct that carried water to power the old mill that once stood along the brook below, when the quarry was active.

The chasm itself is carved out of a marble rock bed. Before it reaches the chasm, Hudson Brook goes over a marble dam (the only one in the U.S.) and then enters the chasm, goes down three or four cascades (one of which is a 8-10 foot slide down a smooth white marble face), continues under a natural marble bridge and then drains out the other side of the chasm. The chasm's white marble walls are sheer and close together.

Waterfall Classification

waterfall - a section of stream or river which falls or slides vertically.

cascade - a smaller version of a waterfall; often used to describe a part of a waterfall. The plural cascades is used to describe a waterfall which is composed of many small drops.

cataract - a very powerful or high waterfall, usually occuring on a river.

chute - a narrow, powerful section of a waterfall, usually found between two large boulders or cliff walls.

74

Connecticut River Valley Region

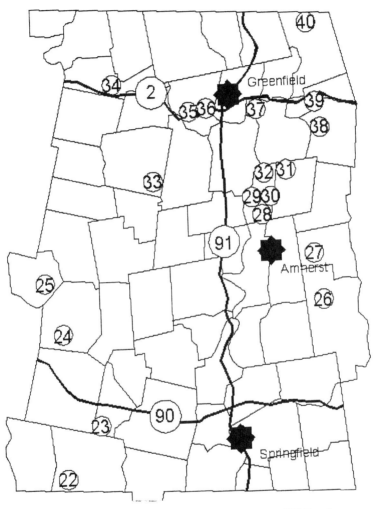

22.	Hubbard River	28.	Gunn Brook	34.	Mill Brook
23.	Pitcher Falls	29.	Slatestone Brook	35.	Sluice Brook
24.	Sanderson Brook	30.	Mohawk Brook	36.	Sluice Brook
25.	Glendale Falls	31.	Roaring Brook	37.	Rock Dam
26.	Hop Brook	32.	Slip Dog Falls	38.	Lynne's Falls
27.	Buffam Falls	33.	Chapel Falls	39.	Briggs Brook
				40.	Pauchaug Brook

22

Hubbard River

Granville State Forest
Granville, MA
Distance: 0.75 mile
Walking Time: 20 minutes
USGS Map: Southwick
Rating: Easy

Directions:

From the Tolland / Granville town line, follow Route 57 east for 0.5 mile to a right onto West Heartland Road. After 0.9 mile you'll come to Granville State Forest. Park just past the bridge on the left, but don't block the gate.

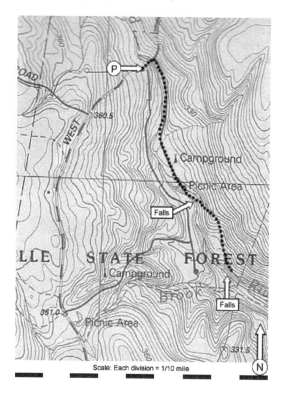

Scale: Each division = 1/10 mile

Hubbard River

Trail Notes:

Walk back over the bridge and take the road to the right, heading downstream. Walk downhill, passing several small cascades. After 0.2 mile, the road begins to pull away to the left, away from the river, and you'll see the fireplaces of the old campsites of an abandoned camping area to the right, between the road and the river. Once through the campsite, the road will return to the river, where the road dead-ends at a traffic circle. Continue on the trail from the traffic circle, and after about 100 yards, the trail forks. Take the right, less used trail to the head of the first fall.

This fall is probably the nicest, although it's only 4 or 5 feet tall. The river here is only 10 feet wide, and seems to have broken through a natural dam. The ledge forming this natural dam is 15 feet high on the left, dropping to 5 feet in the center at the opening where Hubbard River spills through, and steeply back up to 12 feet or more on the right. There is a nice ledge above the pool, but there is no jumping or diving allowed.

Return to the main trail, and continue to the right, heading downstream. You'll pull away from the river, and about a quarter mile past the traffic circle you'll reach another cascade. This cascade is the full 60-foot width of the river, only 12 feet high, but more than 100 feet laterally, almost making a water slide.

Granville State Forest

Visible traces of the early white settlers can be found within this largely unspoiled wilderness straddling the Massachusetts-Connecticut border. An ideal place for hiking, the 2,830-acre Granville State Forest also has campsites, picnic areas and bathhouses along the riverbanks.

77

23

Pitcher Falls

Appalachian Mountain Club
Russell, MA
Distance: 0.75 mile
Walking Time: 20 minutes
USGS Map: Blandford
Rating: Easy to Moderate

Directions:

From the junction of Routes 20 and 23 in Russell, go west on Route 23 for 1.6 miles and take a left onto General Knox Road. Follow General Knox Road for 1.2 miles to South Quarter Road on the right. Parking is 1.2 miles down South Quarter Road on the left in the AMC (Berkshire Chapter) Noble View area. Non-AMC members are requested to leave a donation (see box at parking area).

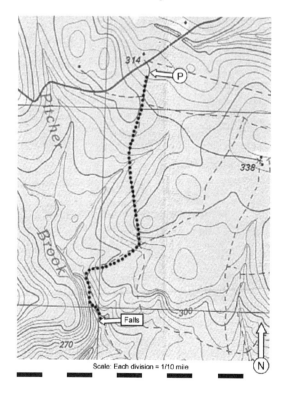

Scale: Each division = 1/10 mile

Pitcher Falls

Trail Notes:

From the parking lot, go past the gate and walk uphill on the dirt access road. In about 100 yards, at the crest of the rise, take a right onto a trail marked with yellow rectangles with a sign indicating Pitcher Brook Trail 0.4 mile.

You'll be walking a wide trail through a mixed forest, with big pines, birch, maple and oaks, and after only 100 feet, you'll begin to descend. After about 200 yards you'll go through a wet area, and the trail will turn to the right and descend a bit more steeply. The trail gets rougher and more narrow.

After about 0.25 mile, you'll cross a small brook. Cross on the rocks, and after a short climb up and over a small rise in an almost all-pine forest, enter a wet stretch in the trail with lots of rock hopping and side stepping, as well as a log bridge.

After 0.4 mile, you'll reach the junction with the Pitcher Brook Trail, marked with white rectangles. Here there are some large pines on either side of the trail, each marked with 3 blue dots. Take the white trail to the right, and down. Now you descend more steeply, and the trail swings right and left on the way downhill. You'll see a series of stone water diverters for erosion control.

After a short level section, where the forest opens up a bit, you'll make another descent and see a double marker on the tree to indicate a turn to the left. Now you are walking along with the brook a short distance to the right. In 100 feet, you'll come to the first of two smaller falls.

The first cascade is about 6 feet, and drops in from the left, flowing to the right around a spur of ledge jutting into the streambed from the left, before swinging to the left again past the spur.

The second fall is only another 50 feet further along. This one is only 4 feet high, and drops into a pool nearly 30 feet across. The pool is fairly deep near the base of the fall, situated in a mini-gorge. There are ledges to left and right of the falls, and you might be tempted to jump from the ledges, but the pool is not deep enough to allow safe jumping. Swimming is OK, however.

Continue past this second fall for 100 yards to Pitcher Falls. The trail brings you to the head of the falls, and you'll need to climb up to the left and go around a knob above the pool to view it from below.

Waterfalls in Winter

Hardy hikers and diehard naturalists may want to try visiting a waterfall in winter, especially during or following periods of sustained and severely cold temperatures. Waterfalls in winter can produce stunning ice sculptures.

However, viewing waterfalls in winter demands an extra measure of caution and preparation. If trail conditions are icy, some type of ice cramp-on is an essential addition to hiking boots. Small, four-toothed instep cramp-ons are inexpensive and can make a slippery descent much safer.

Ice on the moving water of streams and brooks is never safe for crossing. The thickness of ice on ponds and lakes depends on underwater currents or springs, the depth of the water body, natural objects such as rocks and stumps, and daily changes in temperature. There are so many factors that the safest advice is simply *never go out on the ice.*

24

Sanderson Brook

Chester-Blandford State Forest
Chester, MA
Distance: 0.5 - 0.75 mile
Walking Time: 30 minutes
USGS Map: Chester
Rating: Moderate

Directions:

From the junction of Routes 20 and 112 in Huntington, go 4.2 miles west on Route 20 to a parking area (with sign) on the left.

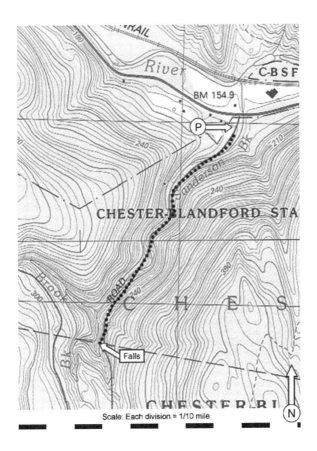

Scale: Each division = 1/10 mile

Sanderson Brook

Trail Notes:

Leave the parking lot and walk to the right, up the dirt road. In about 150 yards you'll cross a bridge with a vehicle barrier, placing the brook on your right. Beyond this point the road is flat and level, and you're walking through the pines. Soon, you will come to a junction with the Newman Marsh Memorial Trail, a 1.5- mile hiking trail through the Chester / Blandford State Forest.

After about one quarter mile, the trail begins a gradual climb to the second bridge. This bridge has no handrails, so take care. There is a small opening to the left now, between the brook and the road. In another 100 yards you'll cross another bridge, placing the brook again on your right. Beyond the third bridge, the road begins to climb a bit steeper. You'll see the brook begin to fall away to the right, as the trail climbs up and left.

A short way beyond the third bridge, perhaps 200 yards, watch for a trail leading off the right side of the road and down into the ravine, marked with a blue triangle, about one-half mile from the parking area. This trail is just after a crossing of a small feeder brook coming in from the left, which may dry up in the summer, but you should also be able to see a brook entering Sanderson Brook from the right, if you look through the trees below.

Now you're on an easy trail, not very wide or steep. Follow for a few hundred yards to the base of the falls. Just before you get to the base of the falls you'll cross a log bridge and a plank bridge.

The falls are in two steps, with the upper piece dropping clean around 12 feet, falling onto a scooped rock and splashing back up about five feet into the air. Sanderson Brook then drops down another 10 feet, splits around a boulder and cascades 20 feet to the pool below before swinging sharply away to the right. If you venture downstream, you will find a few more cascades, as well as the feeder streams entering left and right.

Camping, open fires, cutting or removal of trees or flowers, and littering are all prohibited. Donations to the Massachusetts Conservation Trust are accepted at the parking area, and at the trailhead of the Newman Marsh Memorial Trail.

Types of waterfalls

cascading falls - a waterfall formed by several cascades.

ledge falls - a waterfall formed when a stream flows off the edge of a cliff and free-falls to the bottom of the falls. Often in very low water, a ledge waterfall will shrink to the point where it cascades or trickles down the cliff face. The ledge can curve downstream (convex) or upstream (concave) or not at all (straight).

overhanging ledge falls - often the most impressive and photogenic of all waterfalls. This type of waterfall is formed when the ledge over which the stream flows protrudes out from the rest of the cliff wall, creating an overhang.

slide falls - a waterfall formed by a steeply sloping rock cliff face down which a stream flows.

parallel falls - two waterfalls falling side-by-side

multi-cascading falls - a cascading falls which falls down in many tiny parallel cascades.

fan - a formation created when a narrow cascade spreads out in a fan-like formation at the bottom of a waterfall.

staircase falls - a waterfall which falls in a single stream over many small little edges, creating the image of a staircase.

combination falls - a waterfall which includes features of more than one type of waterfall. For example, a waterfall could cascade at the top and then plunge off of a ledge halfway down. Most waterfalls are combination falls.

25

Glendale Falls

Trustees of Reservations
Middlefield, MA
Distance: Roadside
Walking Time: -
USGS Map: East Lee
Rating: Easy

Directions:

From junction of Routes 8 and 143 in Hinsdale center, go south on Route 8 for 0.8 mile and take Middlefield Road on the left. After 5.3 miles, you'll reach the Middlefield town line where Middlefield Road becomes Skyline Trail. Bear left at the fork, 3.8 miles from the town line, leaving the main way but staying on Skyline Trail. After 1 mile, take a left onto Clark Wright Road. (There's a small street sign here and a sign for Glendale Falls, but these are easily missed so keep your eyes peeled.) Follow this dirt road for 2 miles, until you come to parking on the left.

Trail Notes:

At the back of the parking lot, follow the trail past the sign, and you'll be at the head of the cascade almost immediately. The first cascade is around 10feet high, and is split to left and right across the streambed which is around 30 feet wide. Across Glendale Brook there are the stonework remains of an old gristmill, which you might like to explore after you're done at the falls.

Continue down the trail for 100 yards to the base of the main fall. The trail isn't clearly defined, and there are several possible routes, but for the most part the main trail is to the right of the brook about 20 feet into the woods.

The next cascade is the main fall. It's about 100 feet in height, and there is a fair flow here, spread in a fan falling in two distinct courses to left and right, tumbling down the slope. It is not a huge thundering waterfall, but if you enjoy easy rock climbing and boulder hopping, you'll like this place. The best view is from the large rocks in the middle of the stream below the pool at the base.

Glendale Falls

Fed by more than five square miles of watershed, Glendale Falls is one of the longest and most powerful waterfall runs in Massachusetts. In the spring, the waters of Glendale Brook roar over steep rock ledges more than 150 feet high before joining the Middle Branch of the Westfield River.

The surrounding forest includes hemlock, birch, and beech with an understory of maple, hornbeam, witch hazel, shadbush, and mountain laurel. The 60-acre Reservation was once part of the historic 18th-century Glendale Farm, which operated a gristmill whose foundation can be explored in the woods just north of the falls.

This Trustees of Reservations property prohibits swimming, camping, fires, motorized vehicles, unleashed dogs and firearms. The area is open year-round, daily from sunrise to sunset. There is no admission charge. *Caution:* Seasonal hunting is permitted.

26
Hop Brook

Belchertown Historical Society
Holland Glen
Belchertown, MA
Distance: 0.5 mile
Walking Time: 30 minutes
USGS Map: Belchertown
Rating: Easy to Moderate

Directions:

From Routes 202 and 9 in the center of Belchertown, take Route 9 west for 2.7 miles to a small dirt parking area on the right (north side of Route 9).

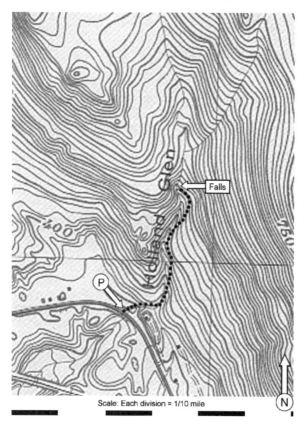

Scale: Each division = 1/10 mile

Hop Brook

Trail Notes:

Follow the white trail blazes of the Metacomet-Monadnock trail through tall hemlocks. This area is protected by the Belchertown Historical Society. You'll pass a house off to the right, and soon come to a crossing over Hop Brook. Soon after the crossing you'll come to the first of some 8- and 10-foot falls.

In this section, you'll find yourself walking through a small gorge, right at the edge of the brook. It's nice and cool here with the water flowing, but in the spring it is buggy. After about 0.25 mile, the trail will veer away from the brook and begin to climb away a bit steeply where the brook bears left. This steep section makes this trail unsuitable for small children. In another 0.1 mile you'll come back to the brook and see the falls.

The falls are about 20 feet high, with the upper section fanning out and flowing over a large boulder, and dropping the last few feet into a pool. You can follow the brook downstream to the head of the gorge and catch a glimpse of another fall.

27
Buffam Falls

Pelham Conservation Commission
Pelham, MA
Distance: 0.25 mile
Walking Time: 10 minutes
USGS Map: Shutesbury
Rating: Easy

Directions:

From the center of Amherst go east on Main Street about one mile to the traffic lights and the junction with North East Street. Cross the intersection and continue straight through, travelling another 1.7 miles, and turn left onto North Valley Road. After about one-half mile, park at the parking area on the left side of North Valley Road (under the power-lines). There is space for several cars.

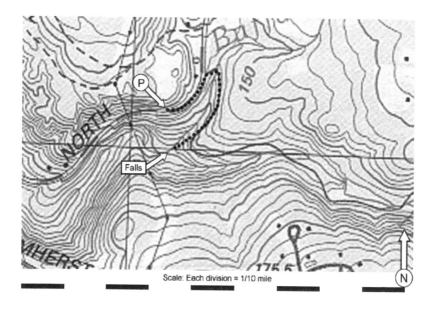

Scale: Each division = 1/10 mile

Buffam Falls

Trail Notes:

Walk north along the road, being watchful for cars. The trailhead is about 400 feet ahead (north), on the right side of North Valley Road. Turn just past a telephone pole with the white trail blazes of the Metacomet-Monadnock trail, just before a house on the left. Almost immediately, you'll come upon a crossing of the Buffam Brook on a wooden bridge. Bear right after the bridge, staying on a wide flat trail through the hemlocks, marked with the white and blue blazes. The flat trail, combined with the short distance, and lack of ledges or other steep drops make this trail a pleasant one for smaller children.

After 100 feet from the bridge, you'll reach the first cascade, which is about 12 feet high, cascading into a pool over a ledge. The bulk of the water fans around to the left, with a small fork off to the right. To get the best view, you'll need to get down to stream level.

After another 100 yards you'll reach the second cascade. The second cascade is smaller, perhaps 8 feet high. It drops over a small 2-foot ledge, then chutes down a long sloping rock from left to right, swirling around in an S shape.

In less than a quarter mile, you'll reach the third cascade just above the confluence of Buffam and Amethyst Brooks. You'll be walking down some steps to the pool below the fall, with a stream on either side. The Amethyst Brook is 15 feet to your left, and Buffam Brook is 10 feet to your right. There are stones and a log laid out around the pool for sitting. The fall here drops about 10 feet, fanning out from 2 feet wide at the top to 8 feet wide when it hits the pool.

The property is managed by the Pelham Conservation Commission. Prohibited are fires, firearms, motorized vehicles, and the removal of rocks and minerals.

28

Gunn Brook

Sunderland, MA
Distance: Roadside
Walking Time: --
USGS Map: Greenfield
Rating: Easy

Directions:

From the junction of Routes 47 and 116 in Sunderland center, go north on Route 47 for approximately 1.5 miles and take a left onto Falls Road. In another mile you will come to Chard Pond on the right, and immediately thereafter you will take a right onto Gunn Cross Road, which is an unpaved road with no street sign. Continue for 0.2 mile to the top of the hill and a small turnout on the right.

Trail Notes:

You can hear the falls as soon as you step out of the car. Climb down on natural steps in the ledge. The fall is in two steps, each about 15 feet, and there is a good flow. There is almost a bit of an undercut behind the fall, but when you cross the stream below on the slippery rocks, you find that the depression doesn't extend behind the falls.

Gunn Brook

29

Slatestone Brook

Sunderland, MA
Distance: Roadside
Walking Time: --
USGS Map: Greenfield
Rating: Easy

Directions:

From the junction of Routes 47 and 116 in Sunderland, go north on Route 47 for approximately 1.5 miles and take a left onto Falls Road. In another 2 miles you will find Slatestone Brook on the right.

Trail Notes:

There is no parking area here, but you can stop at either side of the bridge to step out and take a quick look. There isn't a lot of traffic here. The fall fans out into a beautiful cascade with a fair flow, dropping around 30 feet. The brook soon discharges into the Connecticut River, which is just a few hundred feet beyond the road.

To the right of the stream are remains of an old mill foundation. You can see the stonework of the outer axle support of a waterwheel, and other stonework extends right down to the bridge to complete the whole sluice and spillway.

Slatestone Brook

30
Mohawk Brook

Sunderland, MA
Distance: 1 mile
Walking Time: 30 minutes
USGS Map: Williamsburg
Rating: Moderate

Directions:

From Route 63 in Leverett, turn onto Bull Hill Road. In 0.2 mile, just before the Leverett / Sunderland town line, park on the right in a small dirt parking area for the Robert Frost Trail, with room for two or three cars.

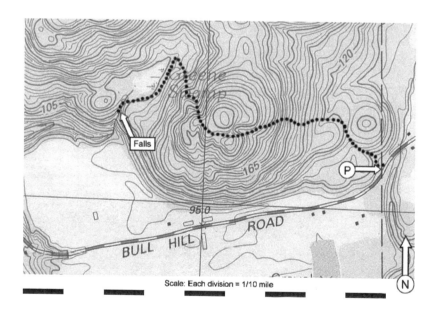

Trail Notes:

Exit the parking area to the left. You'll be on a trail passing through private property. Please stay on the trail and respect the landowners. No littering, removal of objects, or excessive noise please. The trail is open as a courtesy.

Almost immediately, you begin to climb around to the right, and after 100-150 yards you'll reach an intersection with an access trail. Bear right and continue along the orange-blazed Robert Frost Trail (RFT). Cross a wet area in a small hollow, and after 100 yards, take a leftt at a 4-way intersection to continue on the RFT. As you climb, you'll begin to see more hardwoods intrude into the pine forest. After walking about 0.25 mile, just after you crest a small hill, you descend and begin to see evidence of forest thinning.

Just before you reach the thinned area, the trail turns to the left and begins to climb. After you walk up the hill, with the thinned area to the right, you'll be about one-half mile into the walk. You come to the top of another small hill. You won't find a vista, or rocky peak, but it's as high as you'll go. Turn right here opposite a large boulder perched atop the crest, and begin to descend. About 50 yards past the crest, you'll take a sharp right at the first of the signs for The Nature Conservancy's "Greene Swamp" sanctuary. Prohibited are camping, fires, motor vehicles, and removal or destruction of plants or non-game wildlife.

Continue to descend the hill, which has now become quite steep, via a series of switchbacks. When you reach the bottom of the hill, the trail goes away to the right, following a line of ledges. Near the end of the line of ledges, you'll turn sharply left, and shortly afterwards, you'll intersect a blue-blazed trail (the old Clark Mountain Road). The RFT leaves this trail and turns right, heading uphill. Turn left here, and pass a wet area to skirt Greene Swamp. This ATV trail is a wide woods road following the base of the ledges you just descended. This area will be very wet in the spring.

Soon the trail begins to swing around to the right, around the end of Greene Swamp. You'll come upon a trail entering from the left, just before a crossing of Mohawk brook, discharging from the swamp. Just a few more feet along, between the trail and the brook, you'll find a faint, unmarked trail on the left, following along the brook. Follow this faint trail, with the stream on your right, for 150 feet to the head of the falls.

The falls are about 30 feet tall, fanning down over the ledge to splash onto the rocks below. You can cross the brook above the drop-off, and find your way to the base, following a faint trail to the edge of some ledges and descending carefully. Watch your step; this is *very* steep.

Before you leave, sign in at the log book hanging from the tree at the head of the fall, in a waterproof bag.

Roaring Brook

31
Roaring Brook

Mount Toby State Forest
Leverett, MA
Distance: 0.25 mile
Walking Time: 10 minutes
USGS Map: Williamsburg
Rating: Easy

Directions:

Off Route 63 in Leverett, 0.1 mile south of Montague Road, park in the lot on the right, at the sign for guru Ram Das Ashram. There is a box for donations at the trailhead on the right side of the lot.

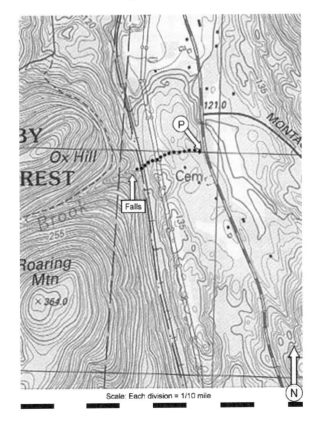

Scale: Each division = 1/10 mile

Trail Notes:

Follow the trail at the right of the parking area. The trail is wide and flat, and soon passes the house. After only a hundred yards or so you'll need to bear left at a fork to stay on the main trail. Pass under some power-lines and enter the pines on a now much narrower trail. You can hear the falls now. You'll emerge from the pines and cross the railroad tracks in 100 feet or so, and the falls are just beyond. *Caution*: Railroad tracks are in use.

The falls are split in two sections with the top section dropping cleanly about 20 feet, and the lower section splitting around a boulder with a few trees growing from it before dropping another 10 feet to the stream below. The ledges and boulders are crossed with trails.

The trail in blue, Roaring Trail, on the left, will take you 1.5 miles to the fire tower atop Mount Toby, but for a shorter trip you can go up this trail for 100 yards and then go left around some large ledges, through a gully or split in the rock, and back to the falls near the base of the upper section. You can sit by the pool for lunch, but the falls are situated in the shadows, a cool and dank spot.

Go around the ledges to your right, following the blue trail. Once you swing around back to the left, and reach the top of a steep climb, the trail descends into a small gully before continuing on. You'll want to turn left here and walk along the top of the ledge. You'll find a faint trail leading to the base of another fall just 50 feet upstream of the first falls. This fall has two drops, each going into a pothole. Even further up is a smaller fall in another pothole. This is worth the extra effort!

Potholes and Plunge Pools

A stream running over an irregular bed develops small whirlpools in many places. Various rocky objects such as sand, pebbles or small boulders can swirl around within the whirlpools and grind deep circular holes. These basins are called potholes. The particles responsible for forming a pothole are often found at its bottom.

Potholes can occur in any kind of rock, and they also come in all sizes. Very large potholes are called plunge pools, and they are commonly found at the bases of waterfalls.

The Falls at Sawmill River

Distance: Roadside;   **USGS Map:** Williamsburg

Directions:

From the junction of Routes 63 and 47 in Montague, follow North Leverett Road 3.6 miles, and take a sharp right onto Rattlesnake Gutter Road. Follow this dirt road for 0.4 mil to Old Millyard Road on the right. Park near the intersection of Rattlesnake Gutter Road and Old Millyard Road.

Trail Notes:

Walk down Old Millyard Road. Although you can see the falls from the intersection, the best views are just a few hundred yards down the road, before you pass the house on the left. The falls are nearly 25 feet high, with a large flow of water, even in the summer months.

The falls are on private property, but you can get some nice open views from the road. Back near the intersection, you can see the remains of the old stonework that was part of the dam and sluiceway that powered the old mill in the era before electricity rendered waterwheels obsolete.

32
Slip Dog Falls

Sunderland, MA
Distance: 1.5 miles
Walking Time: 45 minutes
USGS Map: Williamsburg
Rating: Moderate

Directions:

From the junction of Routes 63 and 47 in Montague, follow Route 47 south for 0.8 mile to Reservation Road on the left. Follow Reservation Road for 0.5 mile to a small dirt parking area on the right, just beyond the gated access road.

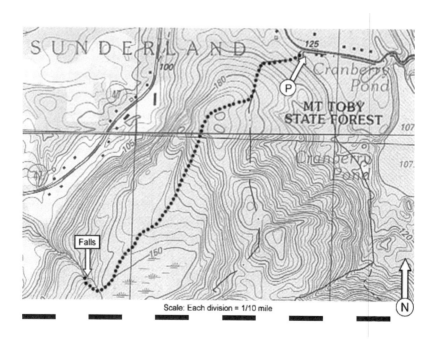

Scale: Each division = 1/10 mile

Slip Dog Falls

Trail Notes:

Exit out the right side of the parking area, past the billboard. Follow the wide trail for only 100 feet to the access road. Turn right and follow the access road for 30 feet to a trail on the left marked with red and blue rectangles.

Begin to climb this wide trail, which is open to bicycles and horses, but not motorized vehicles. You are surrounded by a mixed forest managed by the University of Massachusetts. Shortly after a large deadfall that's been sawed through, you pass a smaller trail leading away to the right and marked in red.

The trail begins to climb more steeply now, and soon another trail comes in from the right. Stay to the left on the main trail, now marked in blue and orange, and now a woods road. After a short level area, where the trail bears to the right and crosses a wet area over some logs, the trail becomes narrower. Next, make a long swing to the left in a damp area loaded with fern, crossing a gully, before turning away to the right again on the other side and beginning a wider stretch.

After another 250 yards or so, the orange-blazed Robert Frost trail leads away to the left. Keep going straight on the blue trail, climbing even more steeply up a stony rise. Once you reach the top of the rise, you're in a mostly hardwood forest, with only a few scattered giant pines. You'll begin to descend gently now, and the trail will become narrower.

Soon you'll reach a triangle junction where you can go right for 100 yards to a small lean-to at the edge of an embankment. Trails lead down the embankment to some interesting caves and ledges. Take a left at this triangle and begin to descend rather steeply on the exposed rock of the trail.

At the base of the slope, you'll pass a trail or two on either side, but keep following the main way, past a bridal trail and an abandoned sugarhouse, and swing right through a wet area which is usually dotted with large puddles. The bugs can be treacherous here, so bring repellant.

100 yards beyond the sugarhouse, bear left at a fork, staying on the blue trail. Just after a wooden bridge over a stream exiting from a swamp on your left, turn right onto a side trail. About 100 yards down this trail, after a long straight stretch, you'll pass the remains of a stone wall on the right, just as the trail curves to the right.

Just beyond this turn, you want to turn off the trail to the right, and head through a small opening in the woods toward the sound of Gunn Brook. Use the sound to guide yourself.

The falls get fairly dry in the summer (as pictured here), but are very nice in the spring. They are about 10 feet high, rolling over and fanning out to 8 feet wide on the way down a ledge with the remains of some old stone work on the right.

Robert Frost Trail

The Robert Frost Trail was conceived in 1982 as a way to link many of the Amherst conservation areas with one grand route. This trail, which now includes such scenic high points as Mount Orient and Rattlesnake Knob, stretches more than forty miles from the Mt. Holyoke Range to Mount Toby to Wendell State Forest. Designated with orange blazes, the RFT is currently one of the five longest hiking trails in Massachusetts. For information, contact:

The Kestrel Trust, P.O. Box 1016, Amherst MA 01004   413-863-3221

33

Chapel Falls

Trustees of Reservations
Ashfield, MA
Distance: Roadside
Walking Time: --
USGS Map: Goshen
Rating: Easy

Directions:

From I-91, take Route 116 west towards Ashfield (exit 25 southbound; exit 24 northbound). About a mile or so before you reach Ashfield center, Route 116 curves sharply to the right. This is where you turn left onto Williamsburg Road and follow it 2 miles, going mostly uphill. The reservation is marked by a clear sign. Parking is anywhere where there is a space near the bridge under which Chapel Brook flows.

Chapel Falls

Trail Notes:

Go across the bridge and follow the road to the left for 50 yards to the trailhead on the left. The trail is a bit steep, and in wet periods it can be quite slippery, so watch your step. In only 100 feet or so, the trail brings you to Chapel Brook at the first of three distinct drops.

The first drop you'll come to is a long sloping cascade about 10 feet in height, but more than 25 feet laterally, like a natural waterslide. In the summer, don't be surprised to find people wading here, although this Trustees of Reservations property prohibits swimming (as well as camping, fires, motorized vehicles, firearms and unleashed dogs).

The next drop is about 12 feet and cascades over a huge sloping rock, fanning out to twice its width by the time it reaches the bottom of the drop.

The third drop is the nicest. It's around 20 feet in height, rounding over the top of a ledge at first, then dropping clean for 10 feet or more to a sloping rock to slide into the pool at the base.

The 173-acre property gets its name from a Methodist Chapel and two-room schoolhouse built here in the early 1800s.

An added bonus is a short loop trail leading out of the parking area, around the western side of Pony Mountain to its summit. A grove of trees gives way to white granite ledges that drop off precipitously, offering unobstructed views south toward the Berkshire foothills. Pony Mountain has a nearly vertical 100-foot rock face (called Chapel Ledge) which offers a challenge to very skilled, technical rock climbers.

This Trustees of Reservations property is open year-round, daily, sunrise to sunset. Dogs must be kept on a leash at all times.

34
Mill Brook

Charlemont, MA
Distance: Roadside
Walking Time: --
USGS Map: Rowe
Rating: Easy

Directions:

From Route 2 in the center of Charlemont, go north on Route 8 for 0.25 mile to Bissell Covered Bridge, and park in a small turnout just beyond. In the spring of 2003, there was a temporary bridge in place just upstream from Bissell Bridge, right over the falls themselves.

Trail Notes:

You will probably hear the falls roaring as soon as you step from the car. The best view is from under Bissell Bridge, and the easiest way there is from the upstream side on the right bank. The way is fairly steep along slippery ledges, but worth the work. The falls are really the remnants of an old stone dam, and drop 20 or 25 feet.

Mill Brook

35

Sluice Brook- Lower Falls

This trip requires a canoe or kayak

Shelburne, MA
Distance: 1 mile
Time: 40 minutes
USGS Map: Greenfield
Rating: Easy

Directions:

From the old Sweetheart Restaurant on Route 2 near Shelburne Falls, go east on Route 2 for about one mile to a right onto Wilcox Hollow. After 0.4 mile, you'll reach the end of the road where there is a place to land a small boat. There is room for 5 or 6 cars to park, but there are boulders blocking access to the small rocky beach, so you'll only be able to launch boats that you can carry.

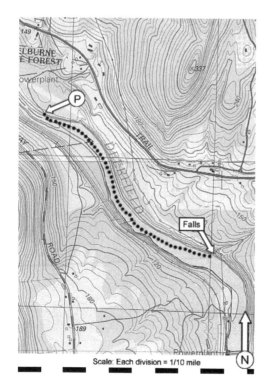

Scale: Each division = 1/10 mile

Sluice Brook- Lower Falls

Trail Notes:

From the rocky beach you will proceed downstream. You'll see several small feeder streams entering from the left and right, some with little falls of their own. There is almost no current here, and the paddling is leisurely. After nearly one mile you'll come to some power lines crossing the river, just beyond is Sluice Brook on your left.

The falls are impressive, about 30 feet high with a large volume flowing. This is a cataract fall, dropping down in a crack in the ledge. The water enters from the right, behind a large spur of rock with a tree growing from it, and tumbles down bouncing left and right making an S turn on the way down.

There isn't much of a place to stop here. While you could beach on the rocks and climb on the ledges, this isn't a place to sit and enjoy a snack. For that you need to cross the river and sit below the power-lines. To return, paddle upsteam back to the put-in.

36
Sluice Brook- Upper Falls

Shelburne, MA
Distance: 1.75 miles
Walking Time: 1 hour
USGS Map: Greenfield
Rating: Easy to Moderate

Directions:

From the State Police barracks in Shelburne, go east on Route 2 for 0.1 mile to a small dirt rest area on the right.

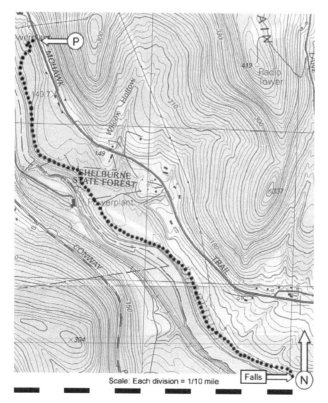

Scale: Each division = 1/10 mile

Sluice Brook- Upper Falls

Trail Notes:

From the parking area, exit out the right end of the area past a sign for the Mahican-Mohawk Trail, and begin on a wide flat trail through planted pines. The trail is marked with yellow disks sporting a green maple leaf, along with the name of the trail, so there's no getting lost here. You'll be walking on a soft bed of pine needles covering the trail.

You'll descend gently in this section, which is a bit damp. There are ferns in the pines, and mosquitoes too, so bring some repellant. Soon after a short zigzag left to right, you'll approach the edge of the Deerfield River valley. There are only a few views from here, but you can see the Gardner Falls power station and river far below.

Follow along the edge of the valley to the left. You'll begin to descend a bit more steeply now. You'll descend quite steeply down a small razor-back to a log bridge spanning a feeder stream, bringing you to the level of the river about one-half mile into the walk. Next, you'll enter an open area with flowers and grasses. Cross the field along a dirt road, to a parking area at the access road on Wilcox Hollow.

Turn right and follow the road for a short way to the boat landing used for the Sluice Brook- Lower Falls walk. Continue past the boat launch, about 0.7 mile into the walk, and now begin a rougher stretch. You'll be going up and down the bank for the remainder of the walk. Sometimes at the level of the river, and other times nearly at the edge of the river valley. Stay on the trail because the land above the edge of the bank is private property.

At two points you'll have to cross over fences on wooden steps crafted for the trail. Soon after the second fence crossing you'll come up to the top of the banking and cross under the power-lines just before they turn to the right and cross the river. You'll go into the trees beyond the power-lines for only a short time before emerging at the turning point on the power-lines.

You could stop in this sunny spot with a nice view of the river, but then continue along for another 50 feet to the falls. The falls are just over a property line, but you can catch a good view while respecting the landowners wishes.

The falls are around 12 feet high. The brook flows in from your left, slicing through the ledge in narrow cracks before taking an abrupt turn toward you to drop over the lip of the ledge and tumble into a small pool. The pool is actually a crack in the ledge, and the far side of the fall is a large sloping ledge, forcing the brook to turn again and exit to your right. Only a few feet further, it tumbles down the lower falls, which aren't visible from the banking.

Salmon Falls and Potholes

Distance: Roadside;   **USGS Map:** Greenfield

Directions:

From the State Police barracks on Route 2 in Shelburne Falls, go west on Route 2 for 0.25 mile and turn left on Maple Street, just past the Sweetheart Restaurant. After 0.2 mile, bear left onto Bridge Street. The Deerfield River is nearly 0.5 mile down Bridge Street, and the falls are just below the Bridge Street bridge. You can park near the bridge along Bridge Street, or turn left onto Deerfield Avenue just before the bridge.

Trail Notes:

Salmon Falls are now only a fraction of their original width in the days before hydroelectric power generation along the Deerfield River, with the falls spilling out to the left side of the dam, on the Buckland side of the river. The plus side is now you can get a much better view of the Potholes in the rocks just below the dam. There isn't any real vantage point from the Buckland side, with the power plant there. The best view is from the other bank, behind the candle company.

The Potholes are amazing. They are natural carvings in the stone, created by the river. Not long ago you could walk along the stones, and check out the holes and canyons, but today access to the river from the Shelburne Falls side is *closed to the public* due to liability concerns. You can access the river from the Buckland side, but you can't reach the Potholes from there. There is talk of reopening the Potholes to the public, due to concerns over lost tourism. Hopefully something will come of the talk, and we can once again walk among nature's carvings.

37
Rock Dam

Turners Falls, MA
Distance: 0.5 mile
Walking Time: 15 minutes
USGS Map: Greenfield
Rating: Easy

Directions:

From the traffic lights on Route 2 in Gill, go across the bridge and through the center of Turners Falls. Pass two traffic lights, and after one mile, bear right onto 11th Street. After 0.1 mile, turn left onto G Street at the four-way stop. Parking is on the left in 0.2 mile, just before a steel gate with a sign for Cabbot Station Fishing Access.

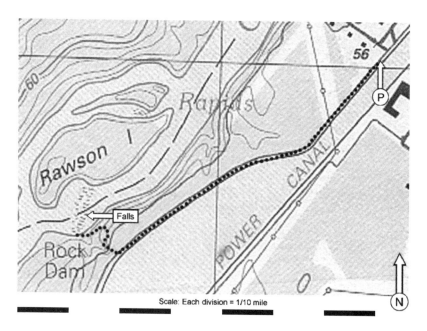

Scale: Each division = 1/10 mile

Rock Dam

Trail Notes:

Leave the parking area and pass the steel gate and another sign, this one for the S. O. Conte Anadromous Fish Research Center, USGS Biological Resources Division. Walk along the pavement for nearly 0.25 mile. You'll be walking alongside the power canal heading toward Cabbot Station. This area is situated on the strip of land between the power canal on your left, and the Connecticut River off to your right. Continue along until you come to a widened area on the road where lines have been painted to allow parking for four cars. Just beyond the guardrails, turn right onto a trail heading away from the power canal.

In just under 100 yards you'll intersect another large trail. Bear right on this trail for only 20 feet or so, and take a left onto a side trail heading down toward the river, near a picnic table. After a short descent, the trail turns left and follows along the right bank of the river. In a few hundred feet the trail forks.

Take the left fork to stay a bit higher up the bank and come out at the far side of the pool below the falls, or take the right fork to continue along closer to the edge of the river. You'll cross an area of rusty looking water seeping out of the banking just before you turn right and cross a bit of wetland on some stones, and emerge from the trees on the ledges just below the falls.

111

The Rock Dam is a natural stone ledge running diagonally across the river between Rawson Island and the right bank. Rawson Island is nearer the far bank of the river, with about 2/3 of the river on the Rock Dam side, and 1/3 of the river flowing on the far side of the island. At a point partway across to the island, water has broken through the dam and is channeled through the gap.

The fall is only 5 or 6 feet, but the flow is awesome, with all the water on the right side of Rawson Island being forced through a gap only 20 feet wide. The fall splits in two around a last remnant of the dam, and you can actually see the river begin to drop even before the water enters the gap. If you walk closer to the gap, you'll begin to see potholes in the rock, carved there by years of erosion.

Below the fall, the river eddies around, making a large pool, before flowing around to the right and sharply left. Across the river you can see where the water from the far side of the island re-enters the river. This is all you can see to indicate an island, from this vantage. Further upstream you can see the lowest bridge over the river, beside the paper mill.

Prohibited are the following: motorized vehicles, camping, fires, littering and alcoholic beverages. The area closes at sunset.

How does moving water turn a water wheel?

Energy is harnessed with water wheels. Every water wheel has a wheel-and-axle machine. Arranged in a circle around a shaft, and fastened to it are buckets, paddles or blades. When a stream of water hits them, they act like levers or cranks to turn the shaft. In this way, the water wheel changes the forward motion of water into rotary motion. All of the older types of water wheels rotate vertically like a Ferris wheel.

The *overshot wheel* works best with a good head of water. Water runs over the top of the wheel; gravity pulls each bucket downward, making the wheel turn.

38

Lynne's Falls

Hidden Valley Memorial Forest
Wendell State Forest
Wendell, MA
Distance: 0.5 mile
Walking Time: 20 minutes
USGS Map: Millers Falls, Orange
Rating: Moderate

Directions:

From Route 63 in the village of Millers Falls in Montague, take Bridge Street for 0.1 mile and take a left onto South Prospect Street. Follow South Prospect Street for one mile and bear right onto Wendell Road at the fork with Mormon Hollow Road. Follow Wendell Road uphill for about two miles; it changes to Montague Road at the Montague-Wendell town line. At the State Forest headquarters building, turn left on a paved access road, and go 0.3 mile to the Ruggles Pond parking area. There is a $5.00 parking fee during the warmer months. You can avoid the fee by parking at the HQ building and walking in.

Trail Notes:

From the Ruggles Pond parking area, follow the white-blazed Metacomet-Monadnock trail into the woods. The M-M Trail descends on a well-worn path. About 300 yards along, you will pass a trail shelter. Lyon's Brook is visible on your left. Pass over a short, wet section of trail and continue descending on a narrower track which is thick with mountain laurel. Lyon's Brook is right next to the trail on your left and offers a view of several minor cascades. After about 0.5 mile, you come to a minor stream confluence with Lyon's Brook. Lynne's Falls is located fifty feet to your right on the smaller brook.

The falls are a series of drops totaling 25 feet over steps in the ledge. The falls are seasonal, and dry up during the dry periods of summer. If you continue on the trail alongside Lyon's Brook another 100 feet, you'll find a faint side trail to another fall where the brook splits around a high spot in the center of the brook.

The Hidden Valley Memorial Forest is owned and managed by the Mount Grace Land Conservation Trust. The land was donated by Mrs. Mable Cronquist in memory of her late husband Dr. Arthur Cronquist, a botanist, author, curator and Senior Scientist at the New York Botanical Gardens. These 66 acres contain dramatic rock formations, Lyon's Brook and Lynne's Falls. There is a loop trail that walks you through three different forest changes -- the Hurricane of 1938, the Gypsy Moth outbreak of 1980, and the logging in 1998. There is also a side trail to an outlook atop Jerusalem Hill.

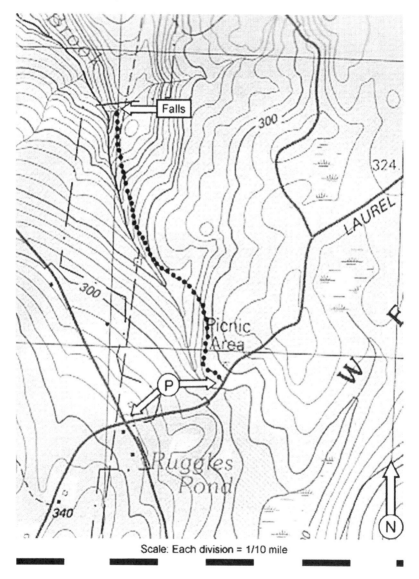

Scale: Each division = 1/10 mile

114

Lynne's Falls

The Metacomet-Monadnock Trail

The Metacomet-Monadnock (M & M) Trail in Massachusetts is a 117-mile continuation of the Metacomet Trail in Connecticut. Commencing at the border of Connecticut-Massachusetts, the trail runs over Mount Tom in the southernmost part, then over the Holyoke range, and turns north along hills in the Connecticut River Valley. The northern part of the trail eventually reaches the summit of Mount Grace in Warwick, then crosses into New Hampshire, and finally ends at the summit of Mt. Monadnock. The best way to make sure that you stay on this trail is to look for white rectangular blazes on tree or signs. If you see double white blazes, this means your about to take a sharp change in direction, so pay attention. The trail also has white metal diamonds placed at trail intersections and road crossings. The trail was conceived by a UMass professor and is currently maintained by local groups and by the Berkshire Chapter of the Appalachian Mountain Club, which can be contacted at PO Box 9369, North Amherst MA 01059 *http://www.amcberkshire.org/mmtrail*

The M & M Trail in Wendell State Forest

There is a 5-mile section of the Metacomet-Monadnock Trail that traverses a variety of terrain through Wendell State Forest. You begin at Ruggles Pond, descending along Lyons Brook, climb a hill west of the Whales Head, and descend to the Millers River via Mormon Hollow Brook, which you ford three times. You may return via Farley Road, Mormon Hollow Road and Jerusalem Road back to Ruggles Pond.

Ample parking is available at Wendell State Forest Headquarters or Ruggles Pond. Leaving Ruggles Pond, you descend north along the east bank of Lyons Brook. You pass a shelter and a spring before viewing the waterfall on your left. Continue downhill until a rushing stream joins Lyons Brook from the right. The trail turns northeast and steeply uphill until it reaches Jerusalem Road. Follow this road south then east. Just beyond some large cliffs, the trail leaves the road and again climbs steeply to a summit. Look for two side trails leading to vistas to the west. After the second vista the trail begins descending. It turns east along Davis Road, this portion of which is closed. It reaches Mormon Hollow Brook and turns north onto Farley Road. Upon reaching the power-line, the trail leaves the road and follows Mormon Hollow Brook towards the Millers River. You ford this brook three times. The trail then follows the Millers River upstream, detours onto the railroad tracks for a while, and again descends to the left bank of the Millers River. Continue until you cross a bridge over the river and enter into the village of Farley, MA. Follow the blazes throught the streets of Farley. The trail reenters the woods along Briggs Brook, below the Northfield Mountain Reservoir. The return route via Farley Road, Mormon Hollow Road and Jerusalem Road is longer, but has significantly less climb.

39
Briggs Brook

Erving, MA - Village of Farley
Distance: 0.75 mile
Walking Time: 20 minutes
USGS Map: Orange
Rating: Moderate

Directions:

From Route 2 in the center of Farley, take Holmes Avenue on the north side of Route 2. Turn onto Wells Street and park at the junction with Cross Street in front of a sign for Farley Ledge. Parking is available for a maximum of eight cars, but extra parking is available across Route 2 on Bridge Street, as indicated on the sign.

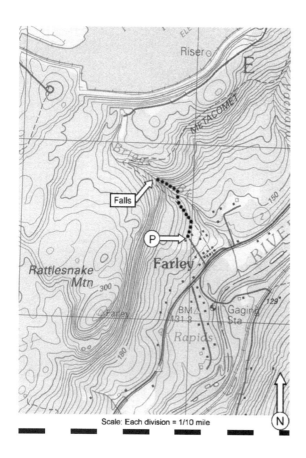

Scale: Each division = 1/10 mile

Trail Notes:

Follow the white blazes of the Metacomet-Monadnock (M-M) trail around two new homes, and bear right at the second house where their driveway splits off to the left. Soon you will cross the brook on a wooden bridge that will be slippery if wet. Here you can view both falls, but a large boulder here offers the best vantage if you want to capture both falls at once.

Another 100 feet brings you to an intersection indicated by two white markers, one over the other. This is a standard turn indicator used on the M-M trail system, where the direction of the upper mark indicates which way to turn. Here you'll bear left and go sharply uphill.

If you go straight here (instead of left), you eventually come to the Hermit's Castle. John Smith, a Scottish immigrant, lived here in the 1800s. He purchased his supplies in Wendell Town, so he wouldn't be found by the residents of Erving. He was later discovered by Samuel Dirth, who was out scouting for a road to his woodlot. Later on, Samuel Holmes, the landowner, befriended the hermit and agreed to let him stay as long as he wished.

Continuing with the directions given on the previous page (going left and uphill), after a few hundred yards of steep climbing, you come to the head of the falls. However, if you go back downhill a short distance and veer off the trail, you will get a better view.

The falls are 15-to-20 feet high and shaped like a veil with a rivulet on the right. In the summer, the veil shrinks away, leaving a cold shower on the right, but the ice formations in the winter are great. An ice cave forms as the freezing water dams and travels left. To explore this ice cave, you can find or break an entrance and climb into a room about 6' X 14'.

About 100 feet further downstream is a second fall which is about 10 feet high. You can visit this fall, but it's all rock hopping. There is no trail here.

From the top of the (first) fall, you can follow the trail a short way to another junction, with branches leading to the Northfield Mountain Recreation Area and some great ledges and caves. One of these caves can be found by following some faint hash marks in the trees to the left of the ridge trail when you get to a dip into a pine-strewn ravine. This cave has two distinct rooms, and the lower room is pitch dark.

Farley Ledge (but not the M-M Trail to the falls) is closed to hiking and climbing from March 1 to July 15, due to the fact that falcons have resumed nesting there, and the intention is to avoid disturbing this protected bird of prey.

The parking area, as well as the trail access itself, is on private property. The landowners permit the use of their land conditionally. They request that you drive slowly and keep the noise level down.

40
Pauchaug Brook

Northfield, MA
Distance: Roadside
Walking Time: --
USGS Map: Northfield
Rating: Easy

Directions:

Right off the junction of Routes 63 and 10, north of Northfield, park in a small turnout on Route 10 near the junction, and cross the road to a small grassy area.

Trail Notes:

This small waterfall of 25 feet is situated at the far end of what used to be the Wanamaker Pond before the dam broke. A good volume flows in the spring, and even in the summer there is a fair flow. The small grassy area at the junction is not the best place to view the fall. For a better view, walk to or park at (but do not block) a small dirt road about 0.1 mile north on Route 63.

The Central Massachusetts / Worcester Region

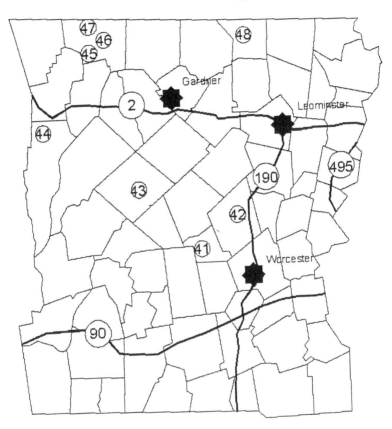

41.   Turkey Hill Brook
42.   Lovellville Falls
43.   Galloway Brook
44.   Bear's Den
45.   Doane Falls
46.   Spirit Falls
47.   Royalston Falls
48.   Trap Falls

41

Turkey Hill Brook

Moore State Park
Paxton, MA
Distance: Roadside
Walking Time: 5 minutes
USGS Map: Worcester North
Rating: Easy

Directions:

From the junction of Routes 122 and 31 in the center of Paxton, follow Route 31 South for 1.2 miles to the main entrance on the right on Mill Street. Follow Mill Street for less than a half mile and park in the second lot, just across from the pond, near the old Chalet foundation.

Trail Notes:

Although there are some naturally scenic parts of this brook, for most visitors the main interest in these cascades is because of the mills built upon them. Moore State Park is the site of one of largest mill villages of New England, and it was established in the mid 1700s.

Visitors can see the restored sawmill (pictured here), as well as the remaining foundation stones of a gristmill just 50 feet upstream, the large near-full foundations of the old tavern and the Eames house just across the access road, the Chalet foundation near the parking area, and the remains of a trip-hammer site a few hundred yards downstream.

There are several trails leading away from the area on either side of Turkey Hill Brook. On one trail around Eames pond, you'll find a bat house and an old quarry on the Stairway Loop trail that will bring you out to the point in Eames Pond. The main access road between Spaulding School House and the mills is paved and suitable for all.

Turkey Hill Brook

Turkey Hill Brook drops 90 feet over about one-quarter mile. The numerous cascades are mostly small in magnitude around three feet, although there are several artifically created cascades that are larger. The natural cascades fall over distinctly layered rock.

The trail out to Artists Overlook (where the photograph here was taken) crosses the brook on a bridge between the gristmill and sawmill. This trail is wide and flat, also suitable for all access, and offers an excellent view of the sawmill and fall. Trail maps are available at the park.

Lovellville Falls

42

Lovellville Falls

Metropolitan District Commission
Village of Quinapoxet
Holden, MA
Distance: Roadside
Walking Time: --
USGS Map: Worcester North
Rating: Easy

Directions:

From the junction of Routes 122A and 31 in Holden, follow Route 31 north for 2.5 miles. Turn left onto Mill Road, go 0.7 mile and park on the right, just before the bridge over Asnebumskit Brook.

Trail Notes:

Cross the bridge and go upstream just 50 feet to a large ledge; it offers the best vantage of this old mill site. The water spills from the side of the old stonework of the sluice, and further downstream goes around a huge boulder. The falls are 10 or 15 feet high, with a fair flow. There is no pond above the old dry laid stone dam, with the sluice being breached long ago. Go back across Mill Road and view the massive stone blocks that are all that remain of the old mill. The bridge is closed, so you'll have to leave the way you came.

This property is owned by the Metropolitan District Commission, and is part of the Wachusett Reservoir Watershed. There is no swimming, wading or fishing allowed, but hiking is permitted.

Galloway Brook

43

Galloway Brook

Cook's Canyon Wildlife Sanctuary
Barre, MA
Distance: 0.25 mile
Walking Time: 15 minutes
USGS Map: Barre
Rating: Easy

Directions:

From the town square in the center of Barre, go southeast onto South Street. This intersection is a bit confusing. You should be driving away from the Town Hall, toward a big church. Upon entering South Street, there is a gas station / mini-mart to the left. After 0.3 mile, you'll see the Massachusetts Audubon Society sign and parking on the left. There is an entrance fee, but the area is not staffed.

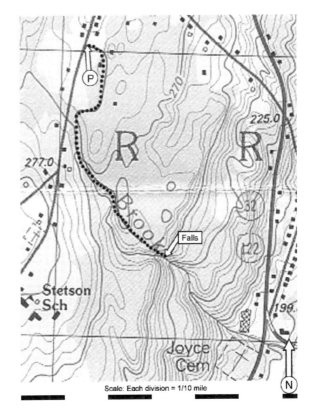

Scale: Each division = 1/10 mile

Trail Notes:

Follow the wide, flat loop trail around to the right, going counter clockwise. The trail is marked with blue markers going out from the parking area, and yellow markers indicate that you are heading back. After 0.25 mile, you'll reach a small pool created by a short dam. Walk to the edge of the ledges and look over Cook's Canyon and you'll see the falls. You can climb down into the canyon to get a better view. Except for this steep detour down into the canyon, this trail is safe for even the youngest children.

The falls are impressive, with a fair flow, but they spread wide and drop about 70 feet. From below, there is no indication of any man-made dam. If you climb down into the canyon, you will find that the sanctuary abuts private property.

Climb back up the steep canyon walls and rejoin the trails, following the yellow markers back to the starting point. You will cross one wet section on stepping stones. This area could be quite buggy in May or June.

Cook's Canyon & Nature Center

This sanctuary, owned by the Massachusetts Audubon Society, includes coniferous and mixed hardwoods bordering the brook, a waterfall, a pond, and more than 100 species of wild native birds. There is a lovely view of the Ware River Valley from Look Out Road. Trails run throughout the property, connecting all of the interesting places. Cook's Canyon is named for the dramatic gorge at the south end of the property.

The Society sponsors organized nature study field trips and nature history workshops.

No public camping is allowed, but there is snowshoeing and cross country skiing in the winter.

44

Bear's Den

Trustees of Reservations
New Salem, MA
Distance: Roadside
Walking Time: --
USGS Map: Orange
Rating: Easy

Directions:

From the intersection of Routes 122 and 202 in New Salem, follow 202 south for 0.4 mile. Turn right onto Elm Street and follow this for 0.7 mile. Turn left onto Neilson Road, and follow this for one-half mile. You will find a turnout on the right where you can park.

Trail Notes:

Walk 100 feet down the trail, where you can see the old stonework of mill buildings off a few feet to the right. Bear left here and cross up and over a small ledge via a split in the rock, and down the other side to the pool at the base of the falls. Here you are in a natural amphitheater, with the cliff behind and to the left, a large spur of rock jutting upward across the river to the right, and the water flowing toward you and turning sharply right and away.

The falls are on the middle branch of the Swift River, where the water is flowing through a 75 feet gorge on its way to Quabbin Reservoir. The water splits around a knob of rock jutting up from the bed of the river. Cross the river and climb the steep rocks to the right of the falls to a nice vantage above.

The land is managed by the Trustees of Reservations, and no fires, camping or motorized vehicles are permitted. *Warning:* Seasonal hunting is permitted at this property, subject to all state and town laws. The Reservation is open sunrise to sunset only.

Bears Den

Bear's Den

On its way to the Quabbin Reservoir, the Middle Branch of the Swift River passes through the steep granite cliffs of Bear's Den. A short trail forks at the entrance, the left spur leading to the gorge, the right leading to the stream bed below the falls. These falls once powered early mills (a long wooden sluice box serving as a flume transported water from the falls, over the river, through a channel cut in the eastern cliff, and onto an overshot water wheel).

According to one local historian, the Bear's Den was a meeting place for Native American tribes. During the summer of 1675, the Indian chief Metacomet (called King Philip by the white settlers) camped at Bear's Den to consult with neighboring leaders and gain their assistance in his campaign against the white invasion of the Connecticut River Valley. Although this story has not been confirmed by other research, it is a well-accepted fact that Metacomet camped somewhere in the local area. Another story tells that the place was named for the fact that one of the first white settlers shot a black bear here.

45

Doane Falls

Trustees of Reservations
Royalston, MA
Distance: Roadside
Walking Time: --
USGS Map: Winchendon
Rating: Easy

Directions:

From Route 2 in Athol, take exit 17 (Route 32) and follow Route 32 north for 2.5 miles, and bear right after you cross the second bridge over the river. Stay on the main way, swinging left. This road becomes Chestnut Hill Avenue. Follow Chestnut Hill Road for 4 miles to the junction with Doane's Hill Road. There is parking on either side of the road.

Trail Notes:

There are a series of falls to the west side of the road. There are three cascades, each with two distinct falls, with a large volume of water flowing. The falls are part of Lawrence Brook, and they drop more than 150 feet on the way to Tully River. The falls range from 10 to 25 feet, and you'll need to go about one-half mile to get to the last one. This is an old mill site, and you'll see many stone foundations and even the remnants of a dam.

The first cascade is just below the bridge and has two falls. Each of the falls are 10 feet, the first coming in from left to right, the other right to left.

The second cascade drops 12 feet, with the left side dropping 8 feet to a sloping rock and angling into the pool below, while the right side drops onto a boulder and sprays up into the air. There are a few trees here, seemingly growing out of the rocks of the streambed. The power of the falls can be felt, even some 50 yards downstream, with a blast of air and spray. Be careful! If you fall in the brook here, you're going for the whole ride. The water is fast, and there's only a few boulders you can hope to slam against to stop yourself.

Doane Falls

The third cascade has two falls. The upper fall drops in a 4-foot step, and then it cascades 25-30 feet, curling counterclockwise into the cliff face, and under-cutting it quite dramatically. The lower fall is about 15 feet high and nearly 30 feet across, dropping clean to thunder into the pool below. The best vantage is from the island below the pool.

With yellow-marked trails on either bank, you can wander here, but there is absolutely no swimming allowed. Be warned -- several people have lost their lives diving from the ledges and drowning after being pulled under submerged ledges by the terrific undertow. There are floats and rope there for emergencies. In the winter it freezes over, giving you only glimpses of the water below. To get the best views of all the falls you'll need to walk the trail along each bank.

This is a Trustees of Reservations property, and there is no swimming, diving, wading, camping or unleashed dogs allowed. The land is named for Amos Doane, who built a mill here in the early 1800s to manufacture doors, sashes and blinds. As early as 1753, Doane Falls provided power for a grist mill, a saw mill, a scouring and fulling mill, and a mill which manufactured pails and tubs. The area is open Memorial Day to Labor Day, 8AM to sunset.

This property is on the new Tully Trail, a 22-mile trail leading out from Tully Lake. The trail takes in Doane Falls, Spirit Falls, and finally Royalston Falls before looping back through Orange, over Tully Mountain and returning to Tully Lake.

46

Spirit Falls

Trustees of Reservations
Royalston, MA
Distance: 0.5 mile
Walking Time: 20 minutes
USGS Map: Winchendon
Rating: Moderate

Directions:

From Route 2 in Athol, take exit 17 and follow Route 32 north for 9.7 miles to the junction with Route 68. Follow Route 68 south for 3.1 miles to a parking area on the right with a sign for Jacobs Hill.

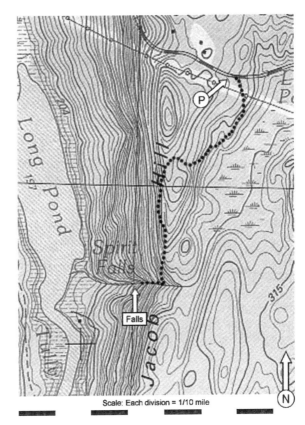

Scale: Each division = 1/10 mile

Spirit Falls

Trail Notes:

The trail is marked with yellow dots. Soon you'll bear right, up and away from the swamp. After you crest the first rise in about 0.25 mile, the trail splits. The left trail is the lower trail which is flatter, but skirts closer to the swamp below Little Pond. If you go right, you will crest Jacobs Hill and come to a vista overlooking Long Pond, before you rejoin the left fork of the trail just above the falls. The total trip to the falls is approximately 0.5 mile. Be advised that you will be skirting a large swampy area, so BRING BUG SPRAY!! The upper trail on the right is further from the swamp and the associated bugs.

If you take the lower trail, the falls are 100 and 200 yards down the slope from the swamp. The slope is fairly steep, so younger children might not get the same level of enjoyment. The falls are a series of cascades, perhaps a total of 150 to 200 feet. The first drop is about 15 feet high, dropping in a few steps. The second fall is about 40 feet, dropping in several steps.

If you continue down, you'll come to the back of Long Pond. At the stream inlet, you can get a nice view of the length of the pond. No houses, no power-lines, peaceful. It looks and feels like you could have just stumbled on a totally forgotten place.

The area you are walking through is a Trustees of Reservations property, and swimming, camping, fires and motorized vehicles are prohibited. This property is on the new Tully Trail, a 22-mile trail leading out from Tully Lake. The trail takes in Doane Falls, Spirit Falls, and finally Royalston Falls before looping back through Orange, over Tully Mountain and returning to Tully Lake.

Jacobs Hill and Harvard Forest

One mile west of Royalston Common, south of Warwick Road (Route 68) is a steep, forested ridge called Jacob Hill. The steep roadway ascending the hill between Falls Road and the center of town is called Jacob's Ladder.

Two miles of trails track the ridgeline of Jacobs Hill, passing through a forest of beech, maple, ash, and birch, and connecting two spectacular westward overlooks from exposed ledges. Both trails take in astounding views of the forested slopes of Tully Mountain, Mount Grace, and the Berkshire Hills. Below is Long Pond and the East Branch of the Tully River, which winds slowly toward Tully Lake. At the eastern edge of the Reservation lies the source of Spirit Falls -- Little Pond, a classic northern bog, whose concentric rings of black spruce and tamarack surround open water and a mat of sphagnum moss.

Spirit Falls is located right along the southern border of Jacobs Hill, so it begins right at the edge of the property of Trustees of Reservation, but it cascades down through land which is owned by Harvard Forest. Its water, which comes from Little Pond at the edge of the Royalston Common, cascades along steep cliffs through a densely wooded area, and finally into Long Pond on the east branch of the Tully River. The falls and 68 acres of surrounding land were given to Harvard Forest in 1963.

Harvard Forest, located in nearby Petersham, is worth a visit if you are interested in the history of land use in Massachusetts. The Fisher Museum of Forestry, named for the founder and former director of Harvard Forest, Professor Richard Fisher, is a wonderful learning experience and offers a series of unique and beautiful dioramas showing the history of the countryside and forestry practices. Harvard Forest was founded in 1907, partly as a response to public concern that the country would soon run short of wood unless forests were managed carefully. Children will love viewing the dioramas, and so will the adults -- there's really nothing like them!

47

Royalston Falls

Trustees of Reservations
Royalston, MA
Distance: 0.75 mile
Walking Time: 40 minutes
USGS Map: Winchendon
Rating: Moderate

Directions:

From Route 2 in Athol, take exit 17 and follow Route 32 north for 11.5 miles to a parking area on the right with a *Trustees of Reservations* sign for Royalston Falls beside the Newton Cemetery.

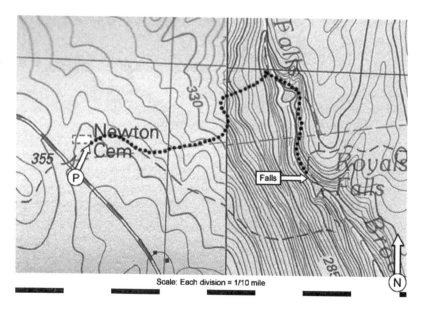

Scale: Each division = 1/10 mile

Royalston Falls

Trail Notes:

Two trails run together as one here -- the Metacomet-Monadnock trail, marked with its familiar white blazes, and the yellow blazes of the Tully Trail. For the first section, nearly a quarter mile, you are on logging roads. The trail has been officially re-routed around a large area of fallen trees. After 0.25 mile, you come back to the original trail where you turn left after crossing a fallen stone wall. Almost immediately the trail forks. The old route bears right; the new relocated section goes left. Bearing left (straight), you climb briefly, then descend a draw toward Falls Brook. A new trail shelter is visible to your left before you ford the brook. After the ford, turn right onto the Tully Trail, following only yellow blazes downstream for about 0.3 mile alongside the brook to the falls. The total length of the trip to the falls is about 0.75 mile, nearly all downhill.

The falls drop into a small gorge, falling some 60 feet. Here you can see first hand the evidence of water erosion, which formed the gorge itself. You can see potholes nearly 50 feet above the stream in an outcrop of rock, where water wore its way through the stone in the early stages of the gorge's development.

137

There are safety cables around the lip of the gorge, but please exercise caution, especially if you are with children. It is possible (for adults) to climb down the gorge for a view from inside. It's fairly steep, and you should assess the risk.

This 217-acre Trustees of Reservations property is on the new Tully Trail, a 22-mile trail leading out from Tully Lake. Entrance to the Reservation is free and open year-round, daily, sunrise to sunset. Regulations: Dogs must be under voice control or kept on a leash at all times. Mountain biking is permitted only on designated trails. *Warning:* Seasonal hunting is permitted.

In 1841, Professor Edward Hitchcock described these falls in his book, *Geology of Massachusetts*. At the time, the falls were popularly known as Forbes Falls because they were located on the property of local farmer Calvin Forbes. Hitchcock wrote,

"The stream is not more than ten feet wide at the spot, but it descends 45 feet at a single leap into a large basin, which from its top had been excavated by the erosion of the water. The sides, to the height of 50 or 60 feet, are formed of solid rocks; now retreating, now projecting; crowned at their summits by trees. Many of these lean over the gulf, or have fallen across it; so that upon the whole, the scene is one of great wildness and interest."

The wild and undisturbed appearance of the falls area today belies the landscape's history. For many years, the land was cleared and farmed. A farmer named Calvin Forbes owned the property in the 1840s, and, for a number of years, the cascade was known as Forbes Falls.

At one time in the past, the owner of the property "improved" the surroundings by building a railing around the falls, with a flight of stairs to go below them, plus seats, tables and swings in the adjoining grove. During the 19th century, Royalston Falls was visited by thousands every summer, and for many years an annual town picnic was held there with musical entertainment. Histories of the area record the existence of a casino building at the top of the falls, where bands played music for dancers. Today, the old staircase is gone, although the Trustees of Reservations installed a cable railing on one edge of the precipitous chasm.

Royalston Falls is one of the more impressive falls in Massachusetts. It has also created one of the more interesting rock formations in the state. The rock over which Falls Brook falls is fairly erosive and has created a chasm with sheer walls into which Royalston Falls tumbles. You can see easily the progression of the falls as it has eroded away and lengthened the chasm.

48

Trap Falls

Willard Brook State Forest
Ashby, MA
Distance: Roadside
Walking Time: 5 minutes
USGS Map: Ashburnham
Rating: Easy

Directions:

From the Ashby / Townsend town line, follow Route 119 west for 0.1 mile to a dirt parking area on the right, near a steel gate.

Trail Notes:

From the parking area, bypass the gate and go up the dirt access road for less than 100 yards to the falls. You won't hear the falls from your car, because Trapfall Brook makes a lot of noise passing under Route 119, but the falls are quite nice.

After you go through the picnic area, with tables, grills, and a restroom, you can cross the foot bridge to view the falls from either bank. The falls split in three and drop 15 feet to the rocks below. The force of the water flowing over the ledge creates a fairly dry hollow behind the falls that you can stand in and get a whole new perspective on waterfall viewing.

The wide flat road, restrooms, and short walk make this an ideal trip for children. Be sure to stop at the ranger station just at the town line for trail maps and information.

Trap Falls

The Metropolitan Boston Region

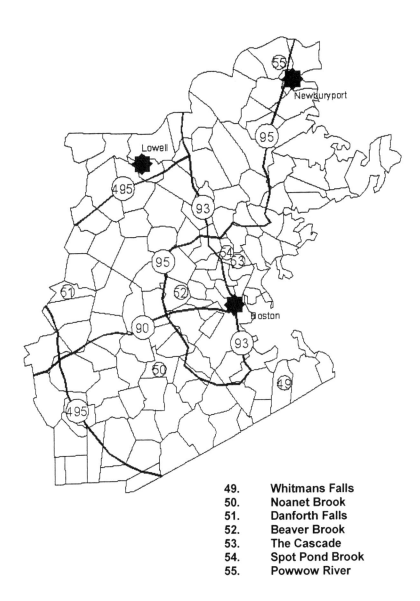

49. Whitmans Falls
50. Noanet Brook
51. Danforth Falls
52. Beaver Brook
53. The Cascade
54. Spot Pond Brook
55. Powwow River

Whitman's Falls

49

Whitmans Falls

Weymouth, MA
Distance: Roadside
Walking Time: --
USGS Map: Weymouth
Rating: Easy

Directions:

From the junction of Routes 18 and 53 in Weymouth, follow Route 53 east for 0.6 miles to Middle Street. Take a left onto Middle Street, and follow for one-half mile, then take a right onto Lake Street. After 0.9 mile, take a right onto Iron Hill Road just before the intersection with Commercial Street. After 0.1 mile, park on the right, just across from a small granite building.

Trail Notes:

Park at the end of the lot, near the herring run. You'll need to cross over the herring run, which is a 3-to-4-foot high cement fish ladder that bypasses the dam at the end of Whitmans Pond. It's only 2 feet across, so a long step is all that's required. You can cross near the dam and hold onto the side of the dam, which is higher than the herring run.

The falls are just beyond. They are about 12 feet high, spilling out between some stonework on the left and ledge on the right. Above, there is more stonework -- the sluiceway for the overflow of Whitmans Pond. It's wooded and damp here, and there are houses just up the banking across the stream.

You need a permit for taking Alewife or Herring, which are issued at the Jackson Square Pool, from April 15 to June 15.

Prohibited here are: throwing objects into the water and interference with the passage of fish.

Noanet Brook

50

Noanet Brook

Noanet Woodlands
Trustees of Reservation
Dover, MA
Distance: 0.75 mile
Walking Time: 20 minutes
USGS Map: Medfield
Rating: Easy

Directions:

From the center of Dover, take Dedham Street east for 1.2 mile to Caryl Park on your right just beyond the tennis courts. From the other side, take Dedham Street for 1.8 miles from the Dover / Needham town line.

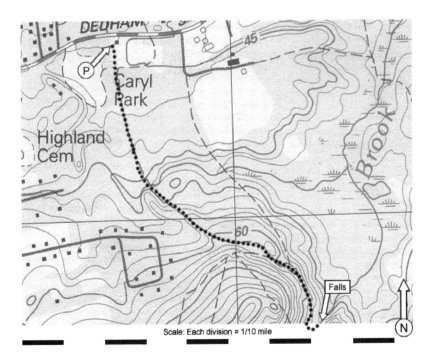

Trail Notes:

Noanet Brook is an old mill brook. In the early 1800s the brook powered a sawmill for the lumber needed to build the homes and businesses in the area. In the mid 1800s, the Dover Union Iron Company, a mill which made wheels, nails and barrel hoops, utilized the power of Noanet Brook via a 36-foot waterwheel. The dam and wheel pit have been reconstructed, and are all that remain after the flood of 1876 destroyed the massive dam and mill.

Caryl Park, the main part of which is to your right, offers tennis courts, a wall for tennis practice or handball, basket ball courts, a ball field and picnic tables. There is parking here for around 40 cars. Admission is free, and the Park is open daily sunrise to sunset, year round.

From the parking area, find the trailhead at a large sign to the left and rear of the tennis courts. There is a large map displayed here with the trails all marked in color. Maps are available to take on your walk. Pass the sign and follow the trail marked in yellow away from the parking area.

In a few feet you'll intersect an access road. Turn right, and go for a hundred yards until the yellow trail turns away to the left. The trail here is wide and flat, covered in woodchips. After about 0.25 mile, when you enter a small opening facing a sign indicating the park boundary, turn to the right and head downhill.

At the bottom of the hill you'll come to a series of junctions. Pass a trail leading off to the left, and go straight on the yellow trail. In another 100 feet, you'll bear left at the next junction, continuing on the yellow trail. Soon you'll pass an iron gate over a culvert.

After about one-half mile you'll enter Noanet Woodlands. Bear left just after the sign, and in just 100 feet or so, bear right on the blue trail. The trail swings around to the left, and you'll pass some horse jumps built of telephone pole sections. Just beyond, you'll enter a clearing, which is a junction point for several trails. The blue trail continues around to the left.

Just down the hill, perhaps 100 yards, you'll hear the sound of the waterfall just as you come to a fork in the trail. Here the blue trail continues up and right toward the highest point on the property, Noanet Peak. At 387 feet, it offers a view of the Boston skyline nearly 20 miles to the northeast.

Bear left and walk down the short side trail to the old mill site. The dam is over 18 feet tall, located at the end of a small grassy clearing. The fall jets out from the sluiceway and drops 20 feet in two steps into the wheel pit. From there the brook seems to disappear, but actually enters a culvert under some trapped deadwood in the pit, to reappear on the other side of the clearing.

The wheel pit is fenced to keep people from falling in, but you can get a good look at it by passing around it and going up the trail on the far side to reach the top of the dam. Here you can see not only the wheel pit, but the lower pond.

This is a Trustees of Reservations property. Trails are open for hiking, cross country skiing and horseback riding. Prohibited are: motor vehicles, camping, fires, trapping, firearms, littering, dogs, alcoholic beverages, and the removal of natural features.

Noanet Woodlands

The Reservation is named after a chief of the Natick Indians, who camped, fished, and hunted along Noanet Brook.

During settlement by white Europeans, Noanet Woodlands was cleared for timber, firewood, and a few small homesteads. In the early nineteenth century, Samuel Fisher, Jr. used Noanet Brook to operate a sawmill, producing boards, planks, and joists for the construction of buildings in burgeoning Dedham. Fisher's business boomed throughout the 1820s and 1830s. Later, the Dover Union Iron Company built a large rolling and slitting mill that made barrel hoops, wheel rims, nail plates, and nail rods from forged iron.

Today, the mill's twenty-four-foot-high dam and twenty-foot-deep wheel pit are preserved, but visitors will have to imagine the towering thirty-six-foot overshot wheel that once powered the mill.

51

Danforth Falls

Hudson, MA
Distance: 0.3 mile
Walking Time: 10 minutes
USGS Map: Hudson
Rating: Easy

Directions:

From the junction of Routes 62 and 85 in Hudson, follow Route 85 north for 0.9 mile. Park at, but do not block, the steel gate on the left.

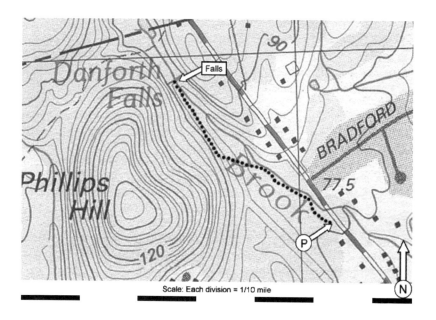

Scale: Each division = 1/10 mile

Danforth Falls

Trail Notes:

Pass the gate and walk along the wide, flat path in the hardwoods. In 100 feet you'll reach Danforth Brook on your right. Bear right where two other trails head away up and to the left, and stay with the brook. Soon you'll begin to climb a bit, and turn towards the right, after a boulder field.

After about 0.1 mile, the trail becomes narrower and smoother. There are a few side trails; some just alternate routes to the same place. Keep to the right-most trail and follow the brook. Soon you'll come to a section where the trail levels out and becomes wider. You'll see some large boulders in the streambed, and some ledges along the banks, where the brook has gone through a small gorge.

Danforth falls is a small cascade falling in a bit of an S curve. They are situated at the boulders at the head of the small gorge. The water flows in from the left, to swing back left and right on the way down the 6-foot drop. The falls slow to just a trickle in the summer, so visit in the early spring for the best view.

52

Beaver Brook

Beaver Brook Reservation
Waltham / Belmont, MA
Distance: Roadside
Walking Time: --
USGS Map: Framingham
Rating: Easy

Directions:

Take exit 28A off Route 95, and follow Trapelo Road east for 3.6 miles to a left onto Mill Road Park. Parking is on the left in 0.1 mile.

Trail Notes:

From the parking area, walk down the short, grassy slope to the Duck Pond. There are picnic tables near the pond, and the park headquarters is off to the left. You can feed the ducks and geese here; they are quite tame. At the left end of the pond, you can take a short trail down either bank of the spill-off from the pond to view the falls. On either side the trail comes to the head of the falls, before continuing on. Cross the paved walkway over the dam to reach the trail on the far side, which continues toward the base of the falls. The trail on the parking lot side loops back around to come up behind the ranger station.

There are two falls here, the upper fall dropping from the sluiceway of the dam creating the pond, and the second just 50 feet downstream, dropping only about 8 feet over the ledges into a small pool below. At this point you are only 200 yards from your car. Return to the dam and follow the trail up to Mill Pond, the site of an 19th century fulling mill. Cross the causeway between the two ponds and return to your starting point.

Beaver Brook

Beaver Brook Reservation

*   (617) 484-6357
*   Open year-round, dawn to dusk

In 1893, this was the first reservation established by the Metropolitan Parks Commission (which later became the Metropolitan District Commission). Beaver Brook Reservation is 59 acres of open fields, wetlands and woodlands. Ponds, fields, marsh, and a cascading waterfall make the park's north section a delightful place to walk or picnic. The more developed south section features ballfields, a wading pool, a bike path and a children's play area. Beaver Brook's historic significance includes reminders of its past; the remains of a 19th century fulling mill, the historic Robert Morris Copeland House (c.1835) and a monument to the Waverly Oaks, perhaps the most famous trees of the 1890's.

Natural history programs are also offered at Beaver Brook, covering topics such as wildlife, the Waverly Oaks, and the ecosystem of ponds, wetlands, and woodlands.

The Cascade

53
The Cascade

Middlesex Fells Reservation
Melrose, MA
Distance: 0.1 mile
Walking Time: 5 minutes
USGS Map: Boston North
Rating: Easy

Directions:

Take exit 35 off of Interstate 93 south, and take a left at the end of the ramp onto Fallon Drive. In only 100 yards you'll come to a stop at the intersection with Park Street (Note your mileage here). Take a right onto Park Street, which becomes North Border Road just before the intersection with Route 28. Cross straight over Route 28, where North Border Road becomes South Street. After 1.3 miles from the stop at the end of Fallon Drive, take a left onto Pond Street. Follow Pond Street for only 0.3 mile and take a right onto Fellsway East. After another 0.3 mile, bear left onto Washington Street. After going 0.7 mile down Washington St., take a right onto Goodyear Avenue and park at the end of the street in a few hundred yards. This is 2-hour parking except Sundays and Holidays.

Trail Notes:

From the end of the street, enter the woods over a small wooden bridge near the sign for Cross Fells Trail. Almost immediately you'll pass a side trail off to your left, but keep straight and continue into the woods in line with Goodyear Avenue. Soon the trail will swing to the right and bring you to the base of the falls.

The falls drop in three steps. The first drop is 4 feet, followed by an 8-foot drop, and ending in a nice 20-foot drop over a vertical semicircular-shaped ledge. There is only a hint of water in the summer, so visit in the spring, during runoff, or be greeted only by damp rocks.

Care for a longer, more interesting route? Exit the parking area to the left, past the sign, and take a left at an intersection just 50 yards up. Cross the street and head up the hill. Bear left at an intersection just at the top of the hill, following the blue-marked trail. Soon you'll pass a trail heading off to the left. You want to take the next trail heading off to the left, a white-marked trail, the White Rock Trail. This trail heads up and over two or three rocky knolls, or Fells, the last of which offer views of the Boston skyline. Continuing along the white trail brings you to a wooden bridge over the stream. Head back the way you came for 25 feet to a side trail heading downhill toward the head of the falls.

If you have the time, you should explore the other trails. Back in your car, go back to Fellsway East and bear left to continue along the direction you were headed. In less than a mile you'll find a parking area on the right, with a large posted trail map of Middlesex Fells. Take a pen and paper to make notes unless you wish to purchase a map.

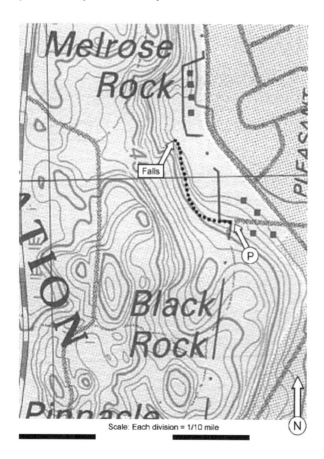

Scale: Each division = 1/10 mile

54

Spot Pond Brook

Middlesex Fells Reservation
Stoneham, MA
Distance: 0.25 mile
Walking Time: 10 minutes
USGS Map: Boston North
Rating: Easy

Directions:

Take exit 35 off of Interstate 93 south, and take a left at the end of the ramp onto Fallon Drive. In only 100 yards you'll come to a stop at the intersection with Park Street (Note your mileage here). Take a right onto Park Street, which becomes North Border Road just before the intersection with Route 28. Cross straight over Route 28, where North Border Road becomes South Street. After 1.3 miles from the stop at the end of Fallon Drive, take a left onto Pond Street. Follow Pond Street for only 0.3 mile and take a right onto Fellsway East. After another 0.2 mile, bear right onto Ravine Street. Park near, but do not block, the steel gate 0.1 mile down Ravine Street, on the left.

Spot Pond Brook

Scale: Each division = 1/10 mile

Trail Notes:

From the parking area, cross Ravine Street and enter the woods on the red-blazed Virginia Wood Trail. You'll immediately begin to climb gently, up a wide, rocky trail. You are in a pine forest with a few scattered beeches, dwarfed by the huge, towering pines. The trail is wide and easy to follow. After a few hundred yards, turn right onto the yellow-blazed Spot Pond Brook trail, just before a stone bridge over Spot Pond Brook.

Follow this trail for less than one hundred yards and pass an unmarked trail crossing a second stone bridge over Spot Pond Brook. Continue along the yellow-blazed trail just around the corner to view the falls, dropping 10 feet over an old stone dam directly underneath the second bridge. You'll need to scramble down the small embankment to get a clear photograph, but you can see well enough from the wooden bench at the lip of the embankment if you just want to sit and enjoy the scene.

156

55
Powwow River

Amesbury, MA
Distance: Roadside
Walking Time: --
USGS Map: Newburyport
Rating: Easy

Directions:

From the junction of Routes 150 and 110 in Amesbury, follow Route 110 east for about 0.5 mile to Main Street. Turn left on Main Street and watch for a sharp right at a traffic light in 0.7 mile where Main Street abruptly turns. After 0.1 mile, turn left onto Friend Street and park in the lot on the right 100 feet ahead.

Trail Notes:

The falls are at the far side of the lot. You'll hear them when you get out of your car. There's a paved walkway along the bank, and across the river you'll find a huge old mill complex, and a courtyard where concerts and other events are held.

Follow the walkway upstream a short way, and you'll find a small dam which may have supplied power to the mills at one time, but if you go downstream you'll soon have to cross the river on a small foot bridge just outside the rear of a restaurant on Main Street. Here you'll get the best view of the falls, which cascade around a small piece of earth, with a few trees seemingly stranded in the midst of the torrent.

The main cascade is about 15 or 20 feet, but the remainder tumbles along under Main Street and the buildings on either side. The banks on either side have been reinforced with stonework to prevent erosion, and Main Street and the mill complex just seems to have built up and over the river. If you take a peek behind one of the mills on the south side of Main Street, you'll see the last few drops in the series of cascades.

Powwow River

Resources

Falls on Old Wendell Road

Recommended Reading

Susan Allport. *Sermons in Stone: The Stone Walls of New England and New York.* NewYork: W. W. Norton, 1990.

Paul Bigelow. *Wrights and Privileges: The Mills and Shops of Pelham, Massachusetts from 1740 to 1937.* Athol, MA: Haley's, 1993.

René Laubach. *A Guide to Natural Places in the Berkshire Hills.* Berkshire House, 1992.

Greg Parsons and Kate B. Watson. *New England Waterfalls: A Guide to More than 200 Cascades and Waterfalls.* Woodstock, VT: Countryman Press, 2003.

Other Trail Guides

The following trail guides describe hikes with references to some waterfalls.

AMC Massachusetts and Rhode Island Trail Guide
Published by Appalachian Mountain Club Books
5 Joy St., Boston, MA 02108

50 Hikes in Massachusetts by John Brady and Brian White
Published by Backcountry Publications
Woodstock VT 05091

Hiking the Pioneer Valley by Bruce Scofield
Published by New England Cartographics
Box 9369, North Amherst, MA 01059

Metacomet-Monadnock Trail Guide
Published by the Berkshire Chapter, Appalachian Mountain Club
Box 9369, North Amherst, MA 01059

Nature Walks in Eastern Massachusetts 2d Edition by Michael Tougias
Published by Appalachian Mountain Club Books
5 Joy St., Boston, MA 02108

New England Hiking by Michael Lanza
Published by Foghorn Press
Box 2036
Santa-Rosa, CA 95405-0036

Sources for Maps

Before venturing out into the wild to look for obscure waterfalls, you will want to consult good, reliable maps. Standard road maps typically show only the major roads. While useful for getting to an area, these are not usually detailed enough to make the final approach to a waterfall. The best maps to get are from the USGS topographic series.

U.S. Geological Survey Maps (USGS)

The topographical maps used as base maps for the hikes in this book are available from many local booksellers or outfitters for about $6.00 each. Each map covers a specific quadrangle (quad) which is named and shown on a state base map. Beginning in the mid 1980s, a new, updated series of USGS maps has been produced, covering twice the area of the older quadrangles. Currently, these 7.5 x 15 minute quadrangle maps, which show elevations and distances in meters, are available for much of Massachusetts. These maps come folded. Maps for the central and southern section of the Connecticut River Valley are still available, but only in the older 7.5 x 7.5 minute format, unfolded. You can order these maps from the sources below. Write, call, or go online to find out current prices and availability.

www.topozone.com

U.S. Geological Survey
> Box 25286, Denver, CO 80225
> 800-ASK-USGS
> *www.usgs.gov/*

Earth Science Information Office
> Blaisdell House, University of Massachusetts, Amherst, MA 01003
> (413) 545-0359
> *www.umass.edu/+ei/esio*

Casimir Pinigis
> 55 Ella Street, Athol, MA 01331
> (978) 249-8486

New England Cartographics
> PO Box 9369, North Amherst, MA 01059
> (413) 549-4124

A.J. Hastings, Newsdealers
> 45 So. Pleasant St., Amherst MA 01002
> (413) 253-2840

Massachusetts Department of Conservation & Recreation (DCR)

As of 2003, the DCR is still offering free printed maps for most State Forests, Reservations and Parks. These are not always detailed, but they do show hiking trails, and they are free and available at each site. Until recently, you could also send an SASE to the DCR and request that certain maps be mailed to you. However, all of this may have changed by the time you read this. At the time of this writing (2003), the status of these maps was uncertain because the old Department of Environmental Management (DEM) was in the process of restructuring itself into a new Department of Conservation & Recreation (DCR), Division of Parks and Recreation.

According to some sources at DCR, there will be no more printing of maps because it is "more cost-effective" to offer the maps online. You can find these maps at *www.state.ma.us/dem/4parks*. However, you may still be able to find old copies of printed maps at individual sites, at least until they run out. For information about the current organizational changes in the DEM and DCR, contact: *www.state.ma.us/dem/index.htm*.

New England Cartographics (NEC)

New England Cartographics publishes trail maps for the Quabbin, Mt. Tom, Holyoke Range State Park (east and west), Mt. Toby, and the Sugarloafs. These are excellent quality contour maps designed for hikers. The maps contain plenty of technical information about the various trails as well as historical facts about each area. Each map costs $5.00, postpaid.

> **New England Cartographics**
> PO Box 9369, North Amherst, MA 01059
> (413) 549-4124
> *www.necartographics.com*

New England Orienteering Club (NEOC)

These maps are highly detailed topographic maps designed for competitive orienteering; they are available for several areas covered in this guide, including Forest Park, Holyoke Range (East), Mt. Tom, Quabbin Hill, and Northfield Mountain. These colored maps display many features not found on other maps, including large boulders and abandoned trails, and are recommended for very experienced map users. For up-to-date information and prices, contact:

> **New England Orienteering Club**
> 48 Holbrook St., Jamaica Plain MA 02130
> 781-648-1155
> *www.newenglandorienteering.org/*

Massachusetts Atlas and Gazeteer

Another source for maps is the *Massachusetts Atlas and Gazetteer,* 1998 (ISBN=0-89933-220-X), published by the DeLorme Mapping Company of Freeport Maine. In addition to providing complete coverage of back roads, this atlas also provides topographic information and listings of various natural features, recreation areas, and historic sites.

Rubel BikeMaps

Rubel's series of Road and Bicycle Maps show all the back roads that are usually part of the trip to a waterfall. Designed for the biking enthusiast, they are great guides to the most scenic drives in Massachusetts. Identified are the locations of all State Parks and Forests, the properties of the Trustees of Reservation and the Massachusetts Audubon Society, major hiking trails, and B&B's. These fold-out maps cost about $5 and cover the following regions: Western Massachusetts, Central Massachusetts, Eastern Massachusetts, plus many others (Boston, Cape Cod, Martha's Vineyard, etc.).

Rubel BikeMaps, PO Box 401035, Cambridge MA 02140
info @ bikemaps.com   *www.bikemaps.com*

Waterfalls at Otis Reservoir (# 8)

Hiking Clubs and Trail Maintaining Organizations

Appalachian Mountain Club: Berkshire Chapter
PO Box 9369, North Amherst, MA 01059
www.amcberkshire.org/

Friends of Quabbin, Inc.
Quabbin Visitor Center
PO Box 1001, Belchertown, MA 01007
413-323-7221
www.friendsofquabbin.org/

Massachusetts Audubon Society
208 South Great Road
Lincoln MA 01773
781-259-9500
www.massaudubon.org/

Metacomet-Monadnock Trail Committee
PO Box 9369
North Amherst MA 01059
http://www.amcberkshire.org/mmtrail

Pioneer Valley Hiking Club
www.geocities.com/pvhcweb/
c/o Wilderness Experiences Unlimited
PO Box 265, Southwick MA 01077

Sierra Club, Pioneer Valley Chapter
100 Boylston St.
Boston, MA 02116
617-423-5775

Springfield Explorer's Club
15 Bruuer Ave.
Wilbraham, MA 01095

Springfield Naturalist Club
c/o The Museum of Science
236 State St., Springfield MA 01103
http://naturalist-club.org/

Land Trusts

The Kestrel Trust
PO Box 1016
Amherst, MA 01004
413-863-3221

Mt. Grace Land Conservation Trust
1461 Old Keene Road
Athol MA 01331
978-248-2043
www.mountgrace.org/

Nature Conservancy: Mass. Field Office
205 Portland St., Suite 400
Boston MA 02114
617-227-7017

Rattlesnake Gutter Trust
PO Box 195
Leverett, MA 01054

Trustees of Reservations
572 Essex Street
Beverly, MA 01915
978-921-1944
www.thetrustees.org

AMC Adopt-A-Trail Program

For information about this volunteer program and
how you can become involved, contact the AMC at:

www.outdoors.org/trails/volunteer/adopt/index.shtml

Author's Web Site for Waterfalls

www.massfalls.com

If you are enjoying *Waterfalls of Massachusetts,*
you might also like to discover the natural wonders of nearby Vermont ...

Hiking Green Mountain National Forest
Southern Section
by Bruce Scofield

New England Cartographics   ISBN 1-889787-06-X   176 pages $14.95

Bruce Scofield's *Hiking Green Mountain National Forest: Southern Section* is a unique introduction to the natural wonders of Southern Vermont. Informative yet entertaining, this book guides the reader to both the popular sites and the little-known destinations, from the evergreen summits of the mountains to the hidden, wild waterfalls; from huge reservoirs to bogs teeming with wildlife. Hikers, walkers, peak-baggers, and backpackers will all find something of interest and value in this comprehensive guide. Filled with accurate topographic maps, photographs, and trailhead directions, this book also tells the story of Southern Vermont through its fascinating history and unusual geology.

What the reviewers say:

This is the indispensable guide for the pathways to our wild hearts in the wild forests and recovering woodlands of the Southern Green Mountains. This guide covers the terrain with ease, providing one-on-one encounters with the trails and paths, natural history and geologic features, spectacular waterfalls and not-to-be-missed views, wildlife and native plants, as well as essential lore on emboldened blackflies. Whether you're a day-hiker with children, an experienced bush-whacker, or a casual "peakbagger" like myself, you'll be reaching for this guide for the nuts-and-bolts on hiking this area -- and for just plain inspiration to get outside.

> Sue Higby, Deputy Director, Forest Watch
> *www.forestwatch.org*

An engaging mix of fact and philosophy; a history lesson as well as a hiking guide. Author Bruce Scofield is always entertaining and educating in his quirky, detailed style. A recommended hiking guide.

> Paul C. Doyle, Jr.
> Nudas Veritas Publications & Vermont Review

Also Available from
New England Cartographics

Maps

Holyoke Range State Park (Eastern Section)	$3.95
Holyoke Range/Skinner State Park (Western Section)	$3.95
Mt. Greylock Reservation Trail Map	$3.95
Mt. Toby Reservation Trail Map	$3.95
Mt. Tom Reservation Trail Map	$3.95
Mt. Wachusett & Leominster State Forest Trail Map	$3.95
Western Massachusetts Trail Map Pack (all 6 above)	$15.95
Quabbin Reservation Guide	$4.95
Quabbin Reservation Guide (waterproof version)	$5.95
Grand Monadnock Trail Map	$3.95
Wapack Trail Map	$3.95
Connecticut River Recreation Map (in Massachusetts)	$5.95

Books

Guide to the Metacomet-Monadnock Trail	$12.95
Hiking the Pioneer Valley	$14.95
Hiking the Monadnock Region	$12.95
High Peaks of the Northeast	$12.95
Great Rail Trails of New Jersey	$16.95
Skiing the Pioneer Valley	$10.95
Golfing in New England	$16.95
Bicycling the Pioneer Valley	$10.95
Steep Creeks of New England	$14.95
Hiking Green Mountain National Forest (Southern Section)	$14.95
Birding Western Massachusetts	$16.95
Hiking the SuAsCo Watershed	$15.95

Please include postage/handling:

$0.75 for the first map and $0.25 for each additional map;
$1.50 for the Western Mass. Map Pack;
$2.00 for the first book and $1.00 for each additional book.

Postage/Handling _____

Total Enclosed _____

(Order Form is on next page)

*Ask about our GEOLOPES -- stationery and envelopes made out of
recycled USGS topographic maps. Free samples available upon request.

ORDER FORM

To order products, call or write:

New England Cartographics
        P.O. Box 9369
        North Amherst MA 01059
        (413) 549-4124
        FAX orders: (413) 549-3621
        www.necartographics.com

Circle one of the following:

Mastercard   Visa   AMEX   Check   Money Order

Card Number _____

Expiration Date _____

Signature _____
Telephone (optional) _____

Please send my order to:

Name _____
Address _____
Town/City _____
State _____ **Zip** _____

Visit our web site
www.necartographics.com